TRANSCENDING ABSENCE

A MEMOIR

BY

Debby Livingston-Jones

EDITORS

Christine Yurko DiRico

Lisa Bechtel and Janet Parsons

Copyright © 2019 by Debby Livingston-Jones

First Edition.

Livingston-Jones, Debby Jean.
Transcending Absence: a memoir / by Debby Livingston-Jones
paperback ed.

1.Families--WV, PA, NH--Memoir. 2.Inspirational—Memoir. 3.Grief—Non-fiction.

Love is Eternal

Love is Powerful

Love is Transcending Absence

ACKNOWLEDGEMENTS

My Daughters; Shelley, Jessica, Kelsey and Tiffany

Thank you for your love, your loyalty, and your forgiveness!

My Son; Chip

Thank you for keeping me humble!

My Grandchildren; Peyton, Elijah, Caiden, Jaycee and Violet

You are proof of God's love. You warm my heart!

Art and Naomi Duprat

Thank you for your tutelage and your love!

My Family at the Unity of Palmyra Church

Thank you for your encouragement and support!

Princess Christine Yurko DiRico

"My most favorite niece that ever lived" – and I quote!

Lisa Bechtel and Jan Parsons

Thank you for your candor and your insightfulness!

For Rosemary

You are my Divine Grace.

Thank you for your love, patience, enthusiasm, honesty
and compassion.

There

I don't really understand absence. Should I? Can I?
Not the loss of the floating leaves on a gusty October day.
No, that's not real absence.
Not the campfire smoke drifting off
into the crisp starlit night air. No, not that either.
No. Not that at all. It's the what ought to be there.
What should be there. What's always been there.
What has to be there. What must be there.

Absence is the loss of who knows you.
Who knows what you've been through.
Whose heart has heard yours pounding.
Whose head has rested on you when they most needed you.
The smile that dove into your heart, exploding like stardust.
I can see it but I want to touch it.

The laughter that made you one.
Absence on the outside, an orchestra echoing on the inside.

Absence. When the moment of midnight comes.
The resounding stroke of the clock.

The cool empty bed beside you.
The loss. Is it the end of today?
Or can it be the start of tomorrow?
We're more than ourselves. We're intertwined.
Enmeshed. Interwoven. Indivisible.
How can that not continue? How can it not always be?
Or can it?

I won't pretend to understand any of this.
Except that absence proves the power of presence.
It underlines it, underscores it. It showcases it, punctuates it.
Absence respects presence; honors it; cherishes it; embraces it;
validates it; vindicates it; without a doubt, it authenticates it.
Absence without presence isn't absence at all.

I once thought I was growing to have wisdom.
Reaching into the cool morning air I now realize the folly of that.
The more you know, the more you know that you really don't know.
No, I don't understand absence.
Should I? Can I? Can we?

By Art Duprat, June 2015

ALSO BY DEBBY LIVINSTON-JONES

in spite of fear
A memoir

2007

In Loving Memory

Of

Sue Snyder Beach

Never Forgotten/Transcending Absence

Terry Clayton Gray, Wanda Tracy, Carol Jean Livingston,

David K. Livingston, Patsy Yeago, Roger Alan Wilson, Cole Hayes

Paul and Gregg Jones, Karen Angney, Jordan Tucker Wilson ,

Lance, Lane and Laronda Golbe, Nina Markham

Believe

INTRODUCTION

Welcome! I am pleased to make your acquaintance!

I'll get right to it. The vein of what you read here grounds itself entirely within the highlighted memory reels of my mind. Just as a photographer might use different lenses to capture an expression beyond the subject, so too, do I use literary countenance to tell my story. Therefore, the words contained herein are a blend of optimism and non-fiction; the nitty gritty truth and transformational mojo. I am the sum of all these and more, and I believe you are too, each of us capable of observing our world in a different light.

My light is not always visible to others. It is a flame tempered by experience, sparked by curiosity, and nourished with imagination. It is my last line of defense of fear and folly and fragility and a few other f-words that fail to dominate it. It is the lighthouse in a sudden storm, and the north star on the path of uncertainty. My light is always available...always ready to lead me further down the road that remains.

Through the smallest of apertures, I can summon and capture a golden ray of sunshine. It penetrates my external identity and in the briefest of moments recharges the most sensitive areas of my wakening soul. Here, I have stumbled upon clues for the mystery of my existence, the real beginning; the start of a long and curious road for a place I cannot describe, yet 'feel' to be familiar; close, but beyond my grasp. This explains 'me' in the greater sense; right brained and left with barely enough tools to navigate my human existence...clumsily...but successfully, nonetheless. What I choose to see isn't always in line with my reality, but in the darkest of times, the light remains.

My story may seem a tad far-fetched at times, but don't dismiss it as fantasy. Like you, I am the product of my experiences...a beneficiary of serendipity and a survivor of mistakes. I have a celebrated life of love, laughter, tragedy, and despair, each and all lending insight and content to the pages ahead. The 'deep' within my psyche is a frequent destination for me, but not my only stop. I surface for a bit of air, occasionally, before I dive back in. I am sensitive to universal laws, and even when I'm not, I abide by them, *as though I really had a choice*

. A good chunk of my life makes reflection difficult, some for lack of memory, others for lack of personal understanding and resolve. Recall can be treasonous to the person I am today, but necessary to show transformation. The greatest gift I have received lies in the distance I've gone to get here. I will be shamefully honest in the way I translate my experiences, but this tale is also meant to entertain; to touch all the senses. My thoughts develop rapidly, but not evenly, where comedy and calamity bear unequal prevalence. I am a product of the Universe, but I am its project, too. Sometimes my need for a no-holds-barred excursion into the ethers overpowers my instinct to be safe. Throw in a teaspoon of blissful naiveté and a splash of benign arrogance, and I'll provide enough rhetoric to engage all your emotional curiosities.

"So-o Hum-m-m"

Don't say I didn't warn you.

Still, I hope you will join me, adventuring through a contemplation within and beyond the five senses. There is much to explore with an arsenal of tools at our disposal, and I will employ some of them. Each of us has so much untapped potential! For example, blind people conceptualize the world differently yet manage to move about with a little help from imagination, intuition and faith, qualities shared by all but limited in use or dismissed altogether by many of us. And yet, they are disabled? I wonder should we all be labeled as such. Each soul is a blessing, each bearing purpose and/or insight for all human possibilities and capabilities. Disabilities help us adapt and expand; to do more with less. We should celebrate disability; not label it. Using the five senses for discovery alone, I believe, is too common a theme for the possibilities we own, and as boring as termites eating their way through a tree.

We will fly over and beyond places you may already have visited, but the spin-doctor who resides in my right brain urges you to take a second look...from a vantage point of faith and wonder, and 'disability'. Take it from a weathered old soul who has mindfully practiced life in these categories; we are all just an undiscovered epiphany away from further potential. Exploration may be necessary for clarity, and evolution will continue in the collective, but for our fear of the unknown, we could take some control over both.

I fancy myself a writer, am inwardly adventurous and well-traveled as such, and I am wise for *whatever good it does to be wise.* Some consider me a little crazy. Some call me 'Mom' which in and of itself gives substance to craziness. I won't disagree because I understand my opinion not to matter much in the grand scheme of things (*and according to my children*). Typically, but not always, I am the eternal optimist in my little human group of friends. No one has ever accused me of being 'non-human', by the way.

I celebrate my victories, but I am not able to rest there. I acknowledge my mistakes, and I am unable to linger there, as well. Success usually begins with a blunder. That's what I tell myself. I laugh and I cry, and I labor over my thoughts. I forgive myself for wrong turns and missed steps, and I amuse myself with whimsy. That said, I christen this trip 'all-inclusive'. The whimsical encyclopedia of my inner child is always at my disposal, and in the willful blink of an eye, I will grab the hand of Peter Pan.

"You have quite the imagination, Debby!" my mother used to say, not particularly in complimentary fashion.

"But, why, Mommy? Where does it come from?" (It wasn't from my mother.)

The Universe beckons.

Here I am.

Here we go.

Grab your head gear and tighten the chin strap.

PRELUDE

As we begin…

…it occurs to me we will need a common language, so let us briefly hover over a few general areas to make our trip more comfortable. This will help get the most out of our time together, provide a foundation for our mutual understanding, and save some time in the process. It contains a brief overview of our background.

Most of us share the same general milestones. We learned to walk around one year of age, cut teeth, and were potty trained shortly thereafter; then started speaking in sentences at two or three. We spent time with family and learned some basic, yet valuable information, like how one might get burned playing with fire, and the potential harm of running with scissors. Our parents and teachers taught us the importance of getting along, and the rewards for scoring 'just a little higher than the other kid'. At some point we learned playground education, too. Survival belonged to the fittest, sissies wore white socks on Thursdays, boys were measured by looks (not intelligence), and our mantra, courtesy of the writers of our constitution *'All men are created equal'* was something we were taught to believe but struggled to witness.

We learned social cues to promote acceptable behavior and we were given boundaries by our parents, our teachers, and our school chums. The rules for each group were not always the same; some of us stayed within the confines we deemed safe and some of us were too overwhelmed by the pulling power of each group to choose sensibly. A few of us acknowledged our parents knew what they were talking about, or so I'm told. *(I haven't personally had such conversation with anyone*

5

in that group). School required 12 plus years deliberation on average, and from there, some of us pursued higher education.

My 'higher education' may have been in a different context than yours.

In our most modest development, we moved from being an individual (*personal identity)* to a connection with others (*a sense of community*). We were encouraged to stretch the little boxes we'd lived in, though some escaped the restrictions entirely. Yet, with all the language and math and science and history we were urged to consume, there was little attention given to our uniqueness, the celebratory gift resonating deep within each of us. So consumed were we with all the important stuff squished into the space of our once vastly open little minds, we became 'no batteries needed' soldiers of diminished imagination. That, or nonconforming outcasts, boldly questioning whatever we'd been told *and suffering the consequences.* One way or another, we clumsily proceeded in patterned and socially acceptable areas, unless of course, we were savants or geniuses or uncharacteristically beautiful.

A small percentage of us went on to great achievements or other noteworthy undertakings...like theatre, politics, or jail. The larger percentage did their best to imitate what they'd learned and are still proudly serving their time on earth...due diligence, and a lofty expectation for someone like me.

Mistakes. (*I just snickered out loud*). By the time we were formally introduced to life outside home, we'd made plenty of those too, just trying to be all the things we were told to be *and weren't*. For many of us, these renderings were mere hurdles, but for others, like me, the blunders were of a greater magnitude, which led to feelings of low self-esteem and the need to disguise my truth, or at the very least put off its detection. Beyond the folds and scars of my extraordinary life, and I found purpose in the most unconventional and/or troublesome places!

6

This story is a testimony. It is about God's love and the forgiving power of the Universe. Before you begin, if you are so inclined, allow a moment to gather and prepare yourself.

Take a deep breath in with me….breathe out…and offer this beneficial chant;

 "So-o-o Hum-m-m"

Ah, yes, I feel better already!

CHAPTER 1

Growing up seven...

...or should I say eight? I was the oldest of seven children, but only by default. My brother Terry died before I was born. The shadow of his absence still lingers, giving life-long reference to the influence for his brief presence on earth. By virtue of my mother's boundless love, I grew to mourn the loss she suffered, and ache for the memories of a big brother I'd never meet. His color-enhanced portrait, completed just three weeks before his untimely death, hung at the center of our living room wall for decades, both to memorialize his shortened life and honor his beautiful spirit. I spent a good chunk of my childhood holding stares with him...and swapping silent conversations, as well.

I don't remember the day I first recognized these musings, nor do I recall how they began. Was it my imagination alone, or did I get a little coaching from my brother on the other side? My earliest memory for these little chit-chats occurred before I started school, perhaps when I was four or five years old. Sitting atop my maternal grandmother's tweed sofa (she called it a davenport), I rummaged through a large photo book I'd found on the bottom of a barrister's bookcase adjacent to the non-working fireplace in her front room. Here, I ran across a picture of him. I knew of Terry's life and death, a result I suppose, of regular graveside visits with Mommy, and early childhood inquisitiveness. What I inherently understood and respected at a very tender age was my mother's suffering. Even as a youngster, it was difficult for me to mention him in her presence.

Chasing memories is no tiny chore for me, and my imagination adds clarity for those reaching the surface. Many are wrinkled thoughts. I stumble through a door in a far corner of my mind, take inventory of a million tattered images, then enhance them, one by one for credibility. One untouched slide reel in my memory, though, is for this brief visit with Momma (Maw-Maw). Momma heard my one-sided conversation and took a moment to sit beside me on the couch, no doubt amused by my story telling.

"This is my brudder" I said to her quite proudly, "he's in heaven."

She smiled and said, "Yes, I know, Debby Jean." She paused and fixed her eyes on me, "I think about him every day. You look very much like him."

Since I rarely felt comfortable speaking of Terry, this must have been a real treat for me. I beamed with satisfaction for the similarities we'd shared, but truth be known there was little to compare. Terry looked very much like my beautiful mother. I was the spitting image of my birth father.

Momma was my maternal grandmother, my hero, and my best friend. I spent a lot of time with her. She wasn't the typical grandma, rather plain except for her strikingly blue eyes and uncommonly tall frame. Very much endeared for her orneriness, Momma was dually respected for her tenacity. She was married and bore four daughters whom she would mostly raise herself. She worked as a waitress in several lunch spots in town. No rocking chair for her, no hair-in-a-bun or frumpy dresses, either. I fondly remember her attire mostly consisting of waitress uniforms and aprons, or polyester smocks and trousers. She had no frilly dresses in her closet, no shoes but those for the comfort of her large feet, and her hair was a beautician's nightmare...short, white, curly, thick, and thoroughly cowlicked. It always looked the same and I never knew her to fuss over it. I wouldn't say she was pretty, well, because she was old to me, but she wasn't ugly, for sure. Momma's beauty was defined by greater attributes than looks, but she had no trouble capturing the hearts of a couple admirers along the way. As for me...well, I adored her.

As a child, I had the wishful notion I was sent to earth to do something really important, sort of like a modern day, girl Jesus. All I needed was a sign from God and I'd set out to save the world. I was a long way from the Red Sea, but on occasion I would accompany Mommy and Daddy to King's Creek to wash the car. I figured Moses had to start somewhere small, too. I imagined all I needed to part the water was to put my faith in prayer. The rocks were slippery *(apparently Moses didn't have to put up with this crap)*, but had they not been there? It was not my only failed attempt to serve the Kingdom of Heaven: I was certain, too, I could heal the dead. I would sometimes practice being dead so I could bring myself to life again *(before someone else died and I made a fool of myself)*. I thought about death more than any child should, I think, and at one point was very close to breaking the *Sacred Covenant* I held with powers greater than me. I was not permitted to talk about it and mostly, I didn't. I still don't, mostly because I don't remember it.

There was a feeling I had, further exemplified by a soft whispering in my ear...I was special, and I didn't doubt it. Not then, not now. However, I do lack hard evidence supporting the notion. Bear with me; there is enough circumstantial stuff in the pages ahead to add credence.

Life 'ever after' was a confusing, yet comforting concept for me, but early on, I did my best to avoid it. It offered too much contradiction. Still, the notion would toy with me in the darkness. If only I could manage to stay out of trouble, maybe I would never have to die. (Then, I remember thinking of what a good person Jesus was and look how that turned out)! Add to my dilemma, someone would claim, *"only the good die young'"* and my fate was sealed. No more girl Jesus stuff for me! Besides, if I

11

were meant to wear sandals, I wouldn't have been prescribed corrective shoes for my flat feet.

The bulk of my childhood, though, was carefree. I loved the outdoors and was, in fact, much to my mother's chagrin, a rough and tumble tomboy: climbing trees, swinging on vines, wrestling with the boys and daydreaming of baseball...always. While other girls my age wore fashionable clothes and make-up, I proudly sported field wear; the only application to my skin was the occasional scrape or bruise with grass stain highlights, and freckles, over which I had no power to diminish. Early on, it didn't bother me much to be different, because I more than made up for my inadequacies in gym class or on the ball field. When teams were picked, I was usually chosen first.

I had lots of friends that were boys...I did not have a boyfriend. Well, there was a time I passed notes in middle school with David, but all that did was provide us a reason to avoid running into each other in the halls between classes or at recess. We were painfully shy. Basically, I had no idea what to do with any boy beyond the note-writing phase (*still don't*), but he was a nice boy, and had I been of a different nature, he'd have been a good catch.

As for my mother, I baffled her. I was well-behaved and people often commented on my good nature, but the difference between me and the rest of the family was hard to ignore. This had been my mother's hope all along, mind you; she professed on more than one occasion she wanted her children to be unique in nature (*be careful what you ask for*), and while she tried very hard to tame any expectations she held beyond us behaving well, she was ill-prepared to deal with my innately born attributes. A mostly quiet kid with a large imagination, I wasn't shy. In fact, I was quite the actor in front of those closest to me. My Aunts (Shirley and Patsy) were amused by my quick wit and immeasurable

12

sense of humor. My Aunt Sally, the youngest of my mother's sisters, was not as easily entertained. She was the closest in age to me and I always felt like I had to try harder to get her attention; when I did, it wasn't the good kind. She came around (or I did). Time would renounce those feelings at some point, and she would become one of my most ardent supporters; one of my best friends.

I do recall some disturbances that rained on my little parade, and others with more penetrating effect. My parents divorced, my birth father moved a thousand miles away and couldn't think of a single reason to stay in touch; my mother remarried, and I was adopted by my stepfather. As a bonus and before it was through, I would become big sister for six kids to follow. My mother was always busy doing while we kids were busy playing, providing substance for most of her 'to do' and 'undo' lists. My father, Daddy, the only father I'd known, was always looking for work. He longed to be employed at Weirton Steel Mill. As it was, he lacked the necessary high school diploma and picked up jobs wherever he could. We lived in a small apartment over a garage on Spruce Street, then moved to our rented home on Pross Street just before I began first grade at Weirton Heights Elementary School atop the hill of the bustling steel mill town of Weirton, WV.

My first-grade teacher thought my lackluster efforts to be the result of laziness, but as I recall, my learning simply played second fiddle to my yearning. My social skills were more erratic than dramatic. I had a timid personality but was hopelessly amused and distracted with fantasies. (*Ornery to a much lesser degree*). The first week of classes I cried for Mommy, and Mrs. Owings grew annoyed with the nonsense. On occasion she'd have me put my head down on my desk so as not to disturb the rest of the class. I'd usually fall asleep, and this was not the punishment she had in mind. My behavior did improve as time went along, but early on, I showed signs of *'if I can't be the best, I don't want to play.'* There was always someone in class outscoring me. I didn't understand it! I didn't like it! There was a time or two I refused to raise my head from my desk. Throughout my life, my competitive spirit continued to provide playful fodder for my younger siblings.

I was rather eager for some areas of learning, though. In addition to a passion for baseball, I had a curiosity for numbers and words, but lacked comprehension in both math and reading skills. Year after year I labored for less than average scores on my report cards. Academically, I may have fared better if I was held back a year or two, but my teachers held great fondness for my mother (they had been her teachers, too, and she had been an exceptional student). I think they just didn't have the heart to tell her of my inadequacies.

My cousin Billy taught me to pitch and catch baseball one summer afternoon in his front yard on Terrace Heights. I was probably around eight years old at the time. He told Daddy how very good a ballplayer I was, and I wanted to play all the time after that. My friends and I enjoyed baseball, stick ball, basketball, dodge ball...mostly on the street but sometimes in our yard. We lived near the top of a steep hillside and as gravity dictates for a downhill field, someone was always running to catch up with an errantly thrown or uncaught ball. I never tired of ball games. I did tire of running after someone else's bad throws, but never to the degree to stop playing.

There was no lack of enthusiasm when it came to the outdoors. I loved to adventure. We made cabins out of sticks in the woods, searched for hidden treasures, whittled tree branches into spears, and spent hours at a time searching the grass for four-leaf clovers. During the day, when the season allowed, we picked apples and peaches from trees in the back yard so Mommy could bake pies, and leaves from a sassafras tree that bordered the woods next to our home; the smell of which left a curious

14

taste in the back of my mouth. We delighted in helping Mommy pick wild black and red raspberries, and one of the first talents I learned from my mother was how to spot a honeysuckle shrub from a quarter mile away.

In the summertime by the onset of dusk, we imprisoned dozens of lightening bugs in old mason jars and sat on the cool earth next to our crabapple tree to make pretend fires with the light they expelled. As a small child, I felt empowered by the evening sky, laying in our yard's nicely manicured grass to absorb more of it. I imagined Terry looking down from the clouds that looked like dogs and bunny rabbits. Most kids, I think, yearn to be older...to grow up and be in charge. I had no such desire. God liked kids better than he liked grown-ups. I was sure of it. In Sunday School, we sang *'Jesus loves the little children'* which validated my thoughts. I heard no such tribute for his love for parents.

Our weekly visits to my brother's gravesite diminished in frequency over the years and I wondered and worried it may have been partially due to my inability to quell my curious nature. This was probably not the case, though. The fact was we didn't have a car much of the time. We relied heavily on others to get us where we were going, and I'm guessing my mother didn't want to take advantage of the kindness of others. I was only about six years old, I guess. I'd always been a Livingston. I'd no recollection of my birth father or the names of any member of his family for that matter. However, the stone marking my brother's grave was 'not' Livingston. "Why does it say Gray, Mommy?" I asked, innocently, after one of our visits.

"That was his name, Debby" she said patiently, offering no further explanation, which, of course, lead to more questions; perhaps more frustrations for my mother.

At home, I was a big sister and played the part well. My younger siblings had difficulty pronouncing my name. They called me 'Dubby' and while I

15

protested, I secretly found it endearing. They were my greatest childhood joy…other than baseball. I felt 'mostly' safe but was afraid of the dark, and troubled by random thoughts of a vast and endless sky. It was as though I might be swallowed up by it. My dead big brother taunted and tormented me at night; *you will die someday, too, Debby'*. Big brothers do things like this, I'm told. In the most noble of my childhood phases, I didn't want to die because I knew it would make Mommy sad.

This is what I told myself, of course, but the bigger truth was how upset I would be if I had to leave Mommy. The sheer fact I remember these things might give a therapist pause but mostly, I believe I was a happy kid.

Until I wasn't.

We moved from our rental on Pross to the other side of Weirton Heights Hill after Dad got his GED and subsequently a well-paying job as a pipefitter apprentice in the tin mill. It was a very exciting and happy time for all of us. The brand-new house was ours (well, the bank owned it, too). It was big and new; easily accommodating for our growing family. "Two bathrooms!!" my younger sister Kimmy loved to exclaim when people came to visit. "And a garage!" blurted my brother Randy.

Life was busy. Mom took to the party line for making money. That sounds a little risqué, but it wasn't. For the times, it was simply a homemaker's dream job. She scheduled parties in women's homes to show off her wares, things like wigs and hair falls, *®Koscot makeup*, and *®Dutchmaid clothing*, the latter being her most successful venture. Dad worked in the mill, full-time, and then, too, as a builder for the same contractor who provided the materials for our new house. He was also a volunteer policeman and a once-in-awhile driver for the P&W Bus Company. I was old enough to stay with my siblings for a couple of hours

16

at a time on occasion. My siblings, in order of their appearance to this juncture, were Randy (born the day our birth father left), Donna, Kimmy and David. I was twelve years old; my mother was pregnant (with Linda) and my life was about to take a series of head dizzying dives, the force of which was so overwhelming, I still suffer the occasional nosebleed.

I made friends easily though my parents were stern about our wandering into the too far in the neighborhood. I never had the feeling they were worried for our safety as much as they were for the imposition on the neighbors, but looking back, I believe my mother might have seized with terror when we were out of her sight. With good reason. It only took one moment for Terry to vanish one early spring day, consequently turning her life upside down. Apparently, I was marked for disaster, too.

Within a few short months of moving to our new address, I was sexually molested by a high school boy who happened to be the older brother of my new best friend. I was horrified, but able to hold myself together enough to hide the terrible truth from my family. I held firm to the belief my mother need not know about it. My best friend witnessed some of it, though. As fate would have it, she told another girl who told her mother, who then called my mother. My relationship with my mother changed, as certain as I knew it might. I was immeasurably embarrassed, ashamed, and simultaneously mortified as my mother looked at me through wet eyes, lips trembling.

Mom couldn't talk to me about it, but Dad did. He did an admirable job, but in hindsight, it would have been better for Mom to talk to me...to comfort me, and to tell me everything would be all right...that it wasn't my fault. She'd lost faith in herself and though I didn't understand it at the time, she was heartbroken for her inability to keep me safe. It had been the way she felt when Terry died, and the fear awakened by this mess seemed to pull her back from me. It was as though she'd lost me too. I'd permanently damaged something of special importance to her: my innocence. For a while, I could not allow myself to look at Terry's picture, either. I wore the shame like a heavy coat and dark sunglasses.

If I were to pick a time my world turned upside down, this was it. I loved my mother and never doubted her love for me, but our relationship was unable to gel as it might have had life been a little gentler to both of us. I was hurt, then angry. I felt alone, and dirty, and small; a splinter in a broken relationship...collateral damage to circumstances for which I, too, had been a victim. Add to my lack of power, the 12 years of my life I'd practiced quieting my voice, trying as hard as my mother to show strength amidst the strain of unrewarded grace and unanswered questions. The 'thing' between us was more complicated than it needed to be. We just never really learned how to talk to each other.

Then, I was a teenager.

I played clarinet in the high school band. Consequently, the only part of high school band I didn't like was playing the clarinet. I loved to march in parades, I lived for Friday night football performances, and the bus trips were always a blast, but I never did quite get the knack of building a relationship with the instrument. Nor did I really try. My mother and father both worked outside the home, their school age children all involved in some extracurricular activity, each of them an added expenditure. Initially, I thought I'd make a good drummer, but girls didn't play drums, which put me off from wanting to join at all. My grandfather was a musician, though, and given the sparkle in his eyes when band signups rolled around, I didn't have the heart to decline. I was greatly enamored by his violin and his saxophone, but he didn't have a spare one of either for me to use. Much to my disappointment, the clarinet was my last and only choice. The dismay was shared by my band instructors for the next six years.

Throughout my teens I was rebellious only as I dared be without getting in too much trouble. I was quiet and mostly unnoticeable by my peers' assessment, though worthy by association of an invitation to an occasional birthday party. So uncharacteristically well-behaved for my age, some of my classmates would later conclude I was one of the smart kids (I wasn't). Theatre may have been the better option than band, I guess.

In my junior year, the band performed for a competition in Parkersburg, WV. Unlike previous overnight trips from home, we were assigned rooms and roommates. Let's just say no one in my group would have picked another to share quarters. But as luck would have it, the competition was long, and we were too exhausted to care about those dynamics...or so I thought...until our room was reported to chaperones for behavior issues. Unbeknownst to me and one of the other girls who'd also passed out from the day's marathon event, there had been some drinking and carousing with an adjoining room of boys. I guess I should have been thankful I didn't awaken with a painted face.

Somehow, I knew my line of defense "but I was sleeping" wasn't going to suffice. 'Somehow' was my mother. Admittedly, innocence hadn't been a regular part of my repertoire, but I hadn't been quite so bold as to break rules of this magnitude. I didn't fear physical retribution, mind you. My mother never needed to raise her hand to me. Her look of disappointment trumped any other disciplinary tactic. This looming punishment in and of itself kept me mostly in line. In truth, I wasn't a bad kid, but a handful just the same. I'd be remiss to deny being a more than a little sneaky and self-absorbed in my teens.

By the grace of God, the guilty parties stepped forward to claim responsibility and to renounce our inclusion. The two girls were kicked out of band. The boys (*if you haven't guessed*) were scolded but as it was at the time and remains to some extent today, *'boys will be boys'* was all the defense they needed.

I digress.

The procedure for descending from my soap box is a work in progress.

CHAPTER 2

My 16th birthday...

...came and went with typical fanfare. As family tradition dictated, we had Mom's home-cooked 'famous to us' spaghetti sauce with freshly baked bread from Weir-Cove Bakery. My cousins, Aunts, Uncles, and Momma all came to enjoy dinner and Mom's chocolate cake to celebrate. Mom was pregnant with my youngest brother Levi. I'd managed to stay out of trouble for a while, and Mom seemed resigned to the fact I wasn't going to get a scholarship for further education. Her dreams for me to be a majorette were also dashed. She continued to get a little testy with me for my tomboyish-ness, but it was just true to my nature, and I think she understood this. Didn't like it but understood it. This was the one part of me I couldn't change if I wanted, and neither could she.

Dreams for my future included joining the Navy, but I had strengths in other areas. I wrote a couple poems for the school newspaper and for the Weirton Daily Times. I was far from brilliant, but somewhat gifted with rhyming and/or passionately penning the occasional story. (I still surprise myself.) The latter phase faded for lack of time when I was hired to work the counter at a little ice cream and sandwich shop called "Van's Dairy." It had been one of my Dad's frequent stops for cigarettes and coffee on his way to or from work in the mill, and after a few chats with Mrs. Van Horn on my behalf, Dad secured me an interview there, the Navy gig still a couple of years in my future.

I loved working there, and I learned an appreciation for maintaining a good work ethic because of my training. Mr. Van Horn was pretty ornery (fact: in today's world he'd have landed in jail for some of his antics), but a kindly young lady named Diane who'd worked there for years took me under her wing. Her doting personality and extensive experience with Mr. Van Horn made certain I was never left alone with him. Mrs. Van Horn was a sweet lady, very tiny in stature, but all business. I'm fairly certain she was aware of her husband's inappropriate advances, but behaviors such as those were often accepted as harmless and part of the social landscape at the time. Due to my experiences with the opposite sex thus far, I began to fear any kind of close contact with older boys or men, except of course, my brothers. I could wrestle with them for hours in our living room or on the front lawn.

I worked at Van's Dairy for close to six months before some mention was made about a persistent sore on the tip of my nose. Another open sore soon took form near my eye and yet another on my lip. Mrs. Van Horn pulled me aside to declare "I'm sorry, honey, it's nothing personal, but we just can't have you working here looking like that. You've been a great worker. Perhaps when these areas clear up, you can come back. Right now, I have to think about my customers."

I was crushed. Embarrassed. Humiliated.

Impetigo? This is what my mother thought.

After months of failed treatment from Dr. Weller, my childhood doctor, a referral to a local dermatologist was scheduled.

At my first visit, the young doctor asked if I'd suffered from any sun burns. We both responded, "No." The truth was, I'd never been burned by the sun. Playing in the sun offered me the most beautiful of brown tans, but I never burned. My siblings all had their share of burnt and blistered skin, but I was largely unphased by the sun…except where my eyes were concerned. I was terribly photosensitive in the bright light. My 'once bright' green eyes had turned less stark and more hazel. They lightened. My vision in the sun without sunglasses was defunct, and though I played ball, my issues with photosensitivity went mostly unnoticed. I simply believed everyone had the same sensitivities and complaining wasn't necessary. While in the outdoors, I would often search out the shady areas when possible, though, and my Aunt Sally, ultimately, suggested my mother have my eyes checked because of habitual squinting.

Since the condition I possessed turned out to be quite rare, most dermatologists didn't recognize it. At the time of my first dermatology visit, most of the patients were, no doubt, teenagers with acne, elderly people with skin tags, and patients of various age suffering other minor skin irritations. Before we were through, the young doctor proclaimed the sun a necessary proponent for growth, but to be cautious with it. He put me on a steroid and gave me antibacterial cream to apply to the areas. Once I completed the prescribed application, he would check me again. He wasn't sold on the cause being a bacterial infection, but one way or another, the diagnosis would reveal itself through the process.

Even through my mindless years (I had more than most), the Universe found ways to get my attention. I would get an otherwise random urge to look for things…to search for information. The word 'cancer' was scary and kind of new to me, but it kept popping up in my thoughts. There were no computers back then and I was completely lost in a library. However, my mother had a collection of *Old World Encyclopedias*. A thought kept nagging for me to look under the section labeled Skin Cancer. I read a very small paragraph about it. The explanation seemed to focus around the elderly, but there was no doubt in my mind I had it. I didn't like what it said, and I didn't mention it to my mother. Had I the chance to have five minutes alone with the young specialist, I believe I might have addressed my concern, but...

I do not profess to being psychic, but I will say I possess a 'feeling of knowing' sometimes. I'm intuitive, I guess. I've struggled with it and diminished its importance through much of my life, but when something heavy is to occur, I am rarely surprised.

In the meantime, I was also being seen by Dr. Weller for different reasons. Unbeknownst to me, my mother was a little concerned with my tomboyish behavior, but I didn't know this at the time of the visit. I thought it was a checkup regarding my delayed menstrual cycle. He took me into the examination room and asked me a series of questions, most of which had nothing to do with the onset of womanhood, then asked me if I hated men.

"NO!" I said, "I don't hate men!" I giggled like a schoolgirl, and immediately felt as immature as I was.

Dr. Weller had quite a reputation in town for being strict and kind of scary. He was not that way with me. In fact, he was quite fatherly. Rumor was he'd offered to adopt my brother Randy and me if my mother was unable to continue to care for us after my birth father left. (I came to believe this was a turning point for my mother—he was somewhat fatherly with her, too, and she had great respect for him). He would go on to tell her (in a rather proud tone) he thought I was a castrating female. I had no idea what he meant, and the dictionary only provided more words I needed to investigate. Anyway, while I was there, he looked at my sore and was certain I had something more sinister than an infection. He had his secretary secure an appointment for me with a reputable dermatologist in Pittsburgh the following month. At first, Dr.

Weller seemed to be very concerned about a condition called Butterfly Lupus. *How could anything with a butterfly in the name be dangerous?*

 More tests came and went, albeit slowly. It was not Lupus, butterfly or otherwise, and we received the confirmation of this just before my appointment with the specialist to occur on the first Tuesday of May, just a year shy of my high school graduation.

Dr. Goldblum's office was on the fifth floor of a small medical complex in the heart of a quickly growing and bustling Oakland District in Pittsburgh, within walking distance to the University of Pittsburgh and several world-renowned medical facilities. Children's Hospital was a block to the south, Montefiore cattycorner from our location, Presbyterian to the North and McGee Women's Hospital less than a mile to the west. Very impressive. Equally scary to a kid from a much smaller town in W.Va. Pittsburgh wasn't a long distance (perhaps a 30-minute drive) but we rarely traveled there.

Fate was in the driver's seat, and there was no surprise (for me) when the doctor rather bluntly exclaimed, "It's cancer..."

My mother, though, became pale, eyelids fluttering. For an instant I believed she may pass out. *Cancer.* Her knees buckled to the side of me, and I grabbed her before she lost her balance.

I felt a tinge of familiarity, as though I'd been in this place before.

"It'll be okay, Mom" was all I could muster, but so concerned was I for her not to collapse, I barely noticed I was being held up myself. I didn't think about it until she stood firm, but I was surprised to turn and see the doctor and nurse in the same place I'd left them...at the other side of the table. Rather than shock or surprise, I remained steady, upright, unafraid...maybe a little daunted. I felt the release of those arms as I turned. It didn't take long for me to realize they must have belonged to Terry.

The diagnosis barely phased me until Dr. Goldblum's instructions; I must never, ever feel the sunlight hit my skin again. A nurse positioned herself next to Mom who seemed not to mind her assistance. The sun, he said, was my deadly enemy. Just a couple of seconds could result in irreparable damage. The injury from past exposure would need to be dealt with over time...and since it was caused by a defective gene, the disorder was irreversible. His warning must have gone on for quite some time, but I was stuck on "no sunlight". *The sun, my enemy? Didn't everyone need the sun to survive? Cover my windows? What is a sunbrella? Wear hats and sunscreen and wrap me in sheets to and from the car? Go outside only at night? No fluorescent lights either? Hmm...does that mean no school? Wait, what about baseball? How could I continue to play ball? No. No. NO!* I quickly activated my 'fight, freeze, or flight' mechanism.

But for a few close calls, a lot of surgeries, topical/medicinal applications and blind faith, I've been running from the diagnosis ever since...

The crueler part of xeroderma pigmentosum was more than I bargained for. It imploded the near vision of my worldview. It was rare...one-in-a-million rare. It was serious, and the spots on my face had to be removed immediately. There would be scarring and no guarantee they could get it all. Plastic surgery. Facial Distortion. The outcome was 'iffy' at best. The surgery would be extensive and hard on my body. Strange as my reaction sounds, I didn't offer up a fight for any of it, except for the preventative instructions. I would rather have died. Put aside my dramatic impulses, add the sunscreen and a hat, and decades later, I'm still fighting the effects of this relentless disease...in and out of the sun.

Xeroderma Pigmentosum, i.e. XP (replace the X with a Z and it sounds just as it looks), is an autosomal recessive genetic disorder that, depending on sub-types, reduces the body's ability to repair UV damaged skin; this is the one common effect for all who suffer from it. People with XP do not receive any more sun damage than the average person, but a break in the chromosome (each parent contributing the same break in said chromosome) of the XP patient limits normal repair. This disorder has left a path of tragedy and despair for too many children and their parents. It also hosts a greater possibility for coupling of other conditions, such as malignant melanoma, hearing loss, poor coordination, loss of intellectual function, neurological issues, and seizures. It is likely to accompany freckling, extremely dry skin and changes in skin pigmentation, and has been linked to other cancers, i.e., blood, brain, eye, throat and thyroid. Life expectancy for many can be less than 30 years. There is no cure, and treatment involves completely avoiding the sun, the latter offering problems of its own. We have been referred to as 'children of the night' since this is the only safe time for us to go outdoors.

I have been hospitalized a dozen times and have had several hundred skin tumors removed, mostly out-patient. The sheer number of these lesions has left it difficult to differentiate between scarring and skin that is untouched. My body has been under siege and under the knife for the better part of my adult life. And yet, miraculously, here I am, well beyond the time allotted for the diagnosis.

On that first day, though...my poor mother. While the nurse prepared me for my first series of shots, Dr. Goldblum led my mother out of the room to give her some more information on Xeroderma Pigmentosum (XP). She returned stone-faced and composed. It would be weeks before I'd learn the bulk of what he told her.

The trip home was mostly quiet but for my plea for a milkshake. She wanted to talk to me, and I knew it, but I imagined, also, the tears she struggled to hold back. I loved the time I spent alone with my mom and was determined to make the most of it, however. I looked forward to the weekly Pittsburgh appointments. I didn't need to talk with her; I just needed to be with her. It felt good to be in her presence even if the circumstances were less than ideal. We left early every Saturday morning to escape the rising sun and be home before it became too potent. Dr. Goldblum's office was situated in the heart of Pittsburgh's Oakland District where he was typically busy treating college and high school students for various stages of acne and/or other skin disorders. His office was equipped with a couple of rooms designated for blue light therapy, and my 6:00 a.m. appointments were scheduled ahead of their use with other patients, as the radiation from the blue light offered a less than healthy chance for me to escape the harmful rays. Dr. Goldblum's demeanor softened with time, and after each visit, he said the same thing. "Be safe! Stay out of the sun and seize the day!" He may have said this last part to every patient, but after a few months, my mind began to overwork a more telling underlying indication.

Treatments consisted mostly of injections of Vitamin B and E, and regular excisions of small pieces of skin sent for diagnosis. If the pathology reports returned 'hot,' the same area sample would be removed with a wider and deeper swath from center sample. The new 'cut' would be sent for further analysis and if any borders remained, the same place would be cut again. This would continue until all borders returned 'normal.' It seemed the size and location for the spots to be totally random, and equally arbitrary as to whether each spot should be biopsied before being treated. Most began as small 'wart-like and pearly' growths which, gone untreated, would break open and bleed. Others presented with brown or black spots. Sometimes, three or four spots were excised; one to be sent for further scrutiny while the remaining two or three were just left to heal over. There seemed to be no medically licensed protocol involved, but I'd assumed the anomaly of the condition to be the reason.

One night, early into my treatments, I awakened a couple of hours after bedtime to hear the faint cries of my mother. I went to check on her. I heard muffled sobs as she spoke into the receiver of the phone hanging from our kitchen wall. My Dad was working the night shift at the mill. She was talking to my Aunt Patsy in Florida, I believe, and I was eavesdropping purely out of concern. Mom choked back tears as she explained what little she knew of the disease, and what little was known concerning it, but what she did know was that children were dying, living only until their late teens or early twenties. "I can't lose another child...I can't!"

I never told my mother what I'd heard, because I couldn't bear to see her suffer...because I couldn't bear to be the cause of her suffering. In fact, my eyes began to well up the moment I heard her crying, and instead of running to comfort her, I quickly retreated to my room. It was just like that with the two of us. I agonized over it. She must have suffered the same helplessness. We couldn't bridge the gap growing between us. *'Maybe someday?'* is what we believed, I guess. Life was just so busy, but through it all, I believed we hadn't given up on each other, and there was that.

I may have been naïve, but I didn't give much merit to the proclamation I was going to die anytime soon. I just didn't know how to convince my mother of the same.

A few months later, we were contacted by a research team from the University of North Carolina. They were growing skin and cell samples of the XP mutation in pathology there and wanted to interview us. They arrived at our home just a few weeks later. Several questions were put forth, and while they were very focused on XP, they had little interaction with me. They asked each of my parents to fill out a form with family history so they could track the DNA break on each side. For a few seconds the room was awkwardly quiet. Finally, my mother explained I was not Dad's biological daughter...they'd tried to find my birth father to no avail (*re;* the adoption process). No-one knew where he was, and all mail sent to known family members had been returned: '<u>NOT AT THIS ADDRESS</u>'.

The leader of the group was quick to proclaim, "No problem...I think we can find him." They asked permission for a sample of my skin and I complied; we wished them well, and they were gone.

Collectively, at this point, I believe we all felt the trip to be a waste of time. There was no way they would find Jerry; our limited understanding of XP left us believe the research was insufficient without him. Our attorneys tried locating him to no avail. Public notices were dispatched to post offices and newspapers in his home state of New Hampshire with no indication he resided there. The efforts to locate him were brought up in court during our adoption (my brother Randy and I had to testify). For all any of us knew, he may have died or moved to Canada.

XP is the result of a broken or missing chromosome, each parent having the same break in the same chromosome (highly unlikely). The research required a sample from each parent.

I graduated from high school the following June (near the bottom of my class). The preceding summer had been both an exciting and tumultuous one for me and my family. My youngest brother Levi was born early in the spring of my junior year, and he was a tremendous joy to me for the months to follow.

Besieged with the weight of a very busy life, Mom was often sick, however. She'd bore eight children, lost one and raised seven, worried over my diagnosis, worked hard at her jobs, and suffered ugly bouts of varicose veins, debilitating her to various degrees. She was frightfully anemic, white as a ghost, and weak, a consequence, I was told, of suffering from Rheumatic Fever when she was a child. When Levi was born, the doctor warned that another childbirth could be too much for her body. (*This hadn't been the first time he suggested it*). She had surgery to remove a build-up of scar tissue, but post-surgery problems ensued. Discharged and home with seven children, two of them toddlers, she couldn't stay 'down' long enough to heal. Back to the hospital, and we nearly lost her.

Dad called me from the hospital. He asked me how everything was on the home front, and I sensed a shakiness in his voice...

"Is Mom okay?" I asked.

There was a short pause before he responded: "I...I don't...I don't think so..." he said, for which I quickly replied. "What do you mean?"

He was crying. "I think we might lose her, Debby."

My first reaction was to pull the phone cord as far as it would stretch. I swiftly turned the corner to the living room desperate to see Terry's picture, but the length of the cord proved too short. Tears formed as panic increased...my voice, though, was steady and unfaltering. I held my breath, then said, "Dad...she won't leave us. She won't, Dad!" But, in my mind, I could see my brother's face, and I silently worried. *If she sees Terry's face, she'll go to him...she'll go with him...NO...NO-O-O!!!* My legs started to quiver, but I held the composure in my voice. "What should I do, Dad?" followed by "What can we do?"

I prayed. I held the picture of my Mother in my head, lying in a hospital bed with all of us around her, Linda and Levi snuggled in beside her,

Donna, Kimmy and David at the side of her bed, Randy and me at her feet. I held this focus for some time. In my mind's eye, I saw her wake up, saying she would be all right. Over and over I did this, as though it was a rehearsal for a major motion picture. I imagined the doctors running into the room to exclaim "it's a miracle!" and "go ahead and discharge her!"

I'd had an experience like this just a few months before...I spoke something...I pictured it, and it came through to reality. I held power in my thoughts...good, bad...otherwise. On that occasion, my thoughts were dark and my mood, vengeful. It was a Saturday and my friends were going to stop by and pick me up for some shenanigans. My mother, though, had errands to run and told me I had stay home with my siblings. I'd kept a watchful eye on my siblings since I was ten years old and thought it reasonable for my brother Randy (just two years my junior) to watch them for the short time she was gone. She responded with "No".

"Why?" I asked, or perhaps demanded.

"Because I said so!" and if looks could kill...

I brooded, of course, waiting for her departure then stomping up the stairs to my room. "This isn't fair!" I yelled at no one and slammed my door.

In the yard outside my window I could hear my sisters playing. Typically, this would have engaged me in a more amused fashion, but my bad energy was highly sensitized in the moment. I was so angry! And then I thought it: 'It would serve her (Mom) right if one of these kids got hurt and she wasn't here!'

A second later, it happened. My youngest sister, Linda, sweet, happy, loving and little more than a toddler, fell hard, landing face first on the cement. I heard Donna's and Kimmy's screams and I ran for the door. Down the steps and through the rec-room I ran, shaking with fear and mumbling through my closing airways "No, No, No, I didn't mean it!"

Linda required stitches leaving a visible scar on her chin. I can still feel the emotional scar of my bad behavior; lesson learned.

My mother didn't come home from the hospital the next day, but she did awaken. By my teenage account, she healed rather quickly. We were all quite excited to see her, but kids have a very short memory when their little world begins to turn again. It didn't take us long to pick up where we left off. Resilience. Busyness. Chaos. Our little kingdom of kids posed little respite for returning to 'as you were.' I guess it was our way of saying 'Welcome Home Mommy," and "we never believed for a moment you were broken...that you would really leave us." Add to our selfish bliss: my mother didn't complain. She wore her life's struggles only in her expressions, her dark brown eyes holding within them not only a pain and sadness too harsh to conceal, but also a spark of hope and optimism. Children see what they want to see...what they need to see sometimes.

Life as the oldest child has its pitfalls, but it also has its perks. I was the oldest of all Momma's grandchildren, and for as long as I can remember, was permitted to sit around the (adult) kitchen table during visits with my Aunts and Uncles. I was enamored with their stories and privy to some things that my siblings and younger cousins might have missed. I was rarely excused, but I believe this was due to the fact I kept my mouth shut. (All things, good or bad, shall pass).

One memory after her hospital stay holds my mother talking about her 'near death' experience. She told us she had crossed over. She and her grandmother, also called 'Momma' were as close as me and my grandmother. Momma Hunt as was her title to us kids told her

"You need to stay strong and go back to your family—it isn't your time, Carol Jean." She went on to say she traveled back through this heavenly tunnel connecting both worlds. She saw a vision of Dave (my dad) sitting at her side, weeping and praying, all of her children standing hopeful vigil around her hospital bed.

Within three days, the ambulance was called again.

According to my Dad, this would never have happened if I'd been less selfish. In truth, I had done a fair amount of whining to attend a sleepover birthday party with a friend. My father emphatically denied, but as was infrequently the circumstance, my mother could (and did on this occasion) overrule in my favor.

Dad was furious with me, and deservedly so. I knew better than to play one parent against the other, and Mom had just come home and needed to recuperate. Still, he said some very hurtful things. "All you ever think about is yourself. If you'd have helped a little more, she wouldn't have ended up back in the hospital!" The words stung, and this was the effect he wanted, of course. I choked back tears, but he wouldn't stop. Ultimately, I snapped, getting the result I sought to volley back the pain. "Don't you dare blame this on me!" I shouted. "The doctors told Mom not to have any more babies after Kim was born!" I caught us both off guard with my remark, but he was visibly taken aback. I was astonished, as well. He obviously didn't realize I knew this truth. *There is a price to pay sometimes, for children to be allowed at the adult table.* Still, we were in each other's face and neither of us was backing down...until we heard Levi crying in the adjacent room.

I hated what he said. I hated my response. I loved my baby brother, Levi, and ran to him.

My mother's hospital stay was brief. She returned home a couple of days later with stern orders from the doctor to rest. She was home less than an hour when my brother grabbed a butter knife in a fit of childish anger and took after one of the girls. This time, though, I was there. Everyone survived.

Over the years, the relationship with my father ebbed and flowed. Into my high school tenure and after my diagnosis, I tested his authority, and his quick, unyielding Scottish temper often got the best of me. Words can't be erased once they fill the air. They can weaken as the wind blows, but even as the particles scatter about the atmosphere into places unknown, they remain capable of taking shape and returning like a boomerang. Each of us could have behaved better, but for this I would continue to fear the most serious of implications for his words; *maybe my mother shared in his opinion of me?* Perhaps it was my age, or I was naïve, or misunderstood, or selfish or all the above, but I couldn't erase the memory of it.

Dad and I did mend, but not wholly. I scaled the wall of self-absorbed teenager into belligerent young adult with lightning speed. My parents struggled to keep our family ship upright while I recklessly delighted in navigating my own way. The two routes rarely merged, and chaos ruled. I delighted in caring for my baby brother, however, and his arrival into my world seemed to slow my downward spiral for a while. The XP provided some issues over the summer (including surgery), but I enjoyed my senior year, in large part due to the smile he offered me whenever I walked into the room.

CHAPTER 3

The earth shifted...

...on a warm and beautiful Spring day. I'd returned from running errands and walked through the back door of our hillside home. My father was on the phone. This wasn't unusual. Our very busy household usually leant to someone being on the phone, but it was immediately clear to me the conversation was problematic. Dad looked at me and gave a nervous smile before he turned his back to continue. "Well, I don't know what to tell you. I don't know what you expect me to say, but if you want to call back la-..." and he stopped. He pulled the phone from his ear as though it had just insulted him. I walked past, rather anxiously, awaiting an explanation for his curious behavior.

"Who was that?" I asked, rather amused by the startled look on his face.

Dad possessed the most charming of 'little boy mischief' smiles, one of his more endearing traits.

I hurried past him to put the groceries away and waited for a response. I turned, but he didn't look at me. His eyes were fixed on his forefinger as it glided across the back of one of the kitchen chairs.

"That..." he started, then paused deliberately before completing his sentence, "that was Jerry."

"Jerry? Jerry who?" I asked, innocently. *(Light bulb) Jerry Gray?*

His eyes glanced at me quickly, and then shifted his focus back to his nervous finger gliding. "Jerry Gray" he confirmed in resignation as though he read my thoughts.

They'd found him. Just ten minutes from the farmhouse in which he was born, the University of North Carolina Research Department had accomplished what my Mother's lawyers, a host of constables, and the postal service could not. In a backwoods little paper mill town of North Woodstock, N.H. situated at the foot of the White Mountains, Clayton D. Gray (a.k.a. Jerry) lived with his common law wife in a cabin he rented from his mother. And...he was just on the phone with my Dad...my father...I mean my other father, Dave.

Now what?

We looked at each other, awkwardly. He was grinning, but not really smiling. I was puzzled by his look. Was he looking to me for affirmation? Was he bracing himself, unsure of my reaction? There was so much going on inside of me, I labored to digest it all. My urge to jump for joy wasn't as great as my impulse to run and bury my head in a pillow which I'd probably have gone ahead and done if my heart wasn't lodged in my throat, and if my firmly planted feet were able to make a move in any direction. I wasn't worried about the words I would say, but I was overly aware of my tone. In an instant, I calmed myself, though. This is clearly me...ever vigilant with my power to temper my enthusiasm if it has any chance to produce an uncertain outcome.

"Really?" I asked cavalierly, "What did *he* want?" (a little too self-righteous with my response). I immediately wanted another chance to respond differently...a do-over.

"He wanted to know what was going on with you and why he had never been contacted about your condition" Dad said, in a slightly apologetic tone.

I never doubted their search for him. When I was twelve years old, I was adopted and given my last name (a formality, really, since 'Livingston' was the only name I knew to use). I sat in the courtroom when various people assigned to the task of finding Jerry gave testimony. I witnessed them swear under oath; they used any and all available means to find the man who'd fathered me. It had been a foregone conclusion he was dead or simply didn't care. So...why now?

The rest of the day came and went with little discussion concerning the call. My mother's reaction was comparable to mine. We stood at three corners of our dining room and looked at each other without saying a word. Three sets of eyes peering at and through each other, trying to ascertain the thoughts behind the veneered gaze thickening the air around us.

I believe my brother Terry to be somewhat amused by the event. Throughout my life, I'd telepathically conversed with him on a multitude of subjects, but this one was new. It was as though I'd deliberately held back any association with our birth father. When I envisioned the two of us, I never connected with him on any level but my own. Throughout my life I pictured him only with the family I knew, and I'd had no memory of my birth father. "Wow, Terry" I mumbled when I retreated upstairs to my room "what are we supposed to do about all of this?"

CHAPTER 4

Before I graduated high school...

...I'd been hospitalized for extended periods of time on two occasions. My first hospitalization was the most serious one. But for my mouth and eyes, my head was wrapped in protective gauze and I looked like a mummy straight out of a horror film. My nose needed the most work as the cancer had infiltrated about a quarter of its structure. Grafting was tricky, and the post-surgical process required packing my nostrils with gauze to reinforce proper healing from the inside, as well. I could only breathe through my mouth, which was difficult enough, but after ten days, they ripped the gauze from inside my nostrils and...well, my eyes still water for the memory of it. The carcinoma on my right temple was deep enough to require skin grafting, too. Flesh from behind my right ear and under my right jaw line was used to reshape my nose and fill the half-dollar size hole lateral to my right eye.

On my second trip, the vermillion line from the middle of my top lip was removed, and a large chunk of my lower lip was excised leaving me a rather palpable crooked smile. I was in the hospital for a week for post-surgical precaution, and another week for another infection.

My roommate was a young lady who had systemic juvenile arthritis. She was a beautiful girl with blonde hair, porcelain white skin and pale blue eyes, a year older than me but much smaller in stature. Her hands and feet were rigidly malformed, and she was bound to her bed/wheelchair.

Her mother or one of the nurses had to feed her because she was unable to chew her food, and she ate a lot of ice cream. She was very personable and sweet, upbeat with a playful demeanor, and she loved to chat, but tired easily, often nodding off in mid-sentence. I was happy for the company but because of the surgery on my lip, talking was a bit more difficult for me; a blessing in disguise.

I most certainly would have said something I shouldn't have. I don't recall her name, but Jennie comes to mind when I think of her. Jennie told me she was in the hospital because she was soon going to die. Frankly, she was so happy and full of herself most of the time, I found this a little hard to believe. She went on to tell me her parents kept insisting she was going to be all right, but she knew better; she'd been suffering for years and was certainly not going to be okay. There was no cure. She said she could see the fear in her mother's eyes.

As for me saying something? For one thing, I'd no idea someone could die of arthritis, juvenile or otherwise, and second, why would they have someone who was about to die in a room with me? (light bulb—Wait...What?) I often speak before I have time to think it through, and when this isn't the case, the words quickly escaping my mouth often result in calamity. It is not one of my more attractive features.

A day or so before I was discharged, Jennie was having some sort of difficulty, but I never learned the source. I awakened from a nap at the sound of the curtain closing between us. There was a lot of shuffling feet and some whispers and mumblings from whom I assumed to be doctors and nurses. Jennie's mother possessed a very worried look in her eyes as she scurried past my side of the room. After some frantic discussion, they hurriedly moved her to another room, and I never saw her again. I didn't ask. I didn't want to know.

The following months were contentious between my parents and me, and Jerry's introduction into my new reality helped stir the proverbial pot. I don't recall being afraid, but I was often moody. I acknowledged my diagnosis but had no real concern for the prognosis, not because I was brave, but because I couldn't hold the focus for it. Being sick without feeling sick is a difficult chore, but there were days I was up for the challenge, taking full advantage of their fears on how to deal with me. Perhaps I was simply a typical teenager, but I'd found self-pity to be an advantageous ally. I'd quietly argue away expectations on their part to be unrealistic for my non-existent future...without saying it. Each time they tried to propel my thoughts for living 'beyond' my medical prediction, I showed my discontent by behaving badly and sublimating their encouragement by 'not feeling myself'. Besides, I was quite happy to stay home with my baby brother and little sister, cheering on my other siblings through their various challenges and triumphs. I played a pretty good martyr.

Unbeknownst to me at the time, Mom had been a little uncomfortable with me caring for Levi. People would often stop us in the grocery store, Levi on my hip, and ask if he was my baby. I beamed with pride. He was a beautiful little boy and his bashful little smile grabbed the attention of more than one passerby. So attached were we, he would often reach for me instead of her. I was smitten, of course. My mother might have felt a little left out, but I just didn't recognize it. She would admit to this many years later in one of our attempts to heal our fractured relationship, and the truth of it gave me a perspective I'd missed.

My Aunt Jean (Dad's older sister) came to visit one day and without any objection from my parents, I went to her Mentor-on-the-Lake home for a couple of weeks. I'd stayed there before, a few days here and a few days there, but never for this length of time. I loved going, but it usually took some pleading with my parents. My cousin, Maggie, a little older than I, took on the role of big sister. I looked up to her, mostly because she was very cool but also because she never asked me to change. She seemed to accept and enjoy my company despite my lack of girly-ness. She picked on me too. In an oddly gratifying way, I liked the attention.

In a constant state of denial, I was otherwise outwardly unscathed by the XP nightmare. My plans didn't include it. I discussed my prognosis with no one. Even my best friends knew little about my situation. I don't recall any fears floating to the surface, but I did feel cheated. After all, I had only a couple of dreams in my arsenal of future goals, and each of them required me to live beyond the time I was given; each of them included a life outdoors. My dreams for joining the Navy were doused.

Upon my return home from my visit, I began waitressing at the Diner in town, but within a few weeks my mother handed me a brochure for airline school. I quickly dismissed the notion, but curiously, almost suddenly, she started urging me to apply for a trade school, get a good job, make something of myself. What changed? I scoffed at the idea, convinced I was a fledgling young adult with one foot stuck in the box, and another in the grave, and nothing noteworthy to put on my marker. *Oh-h the shame!* Drama aside, I was convinced it was another way for them to hide the truth from me, and I was quietly frustrated with their ridiculous attempts to push me out of the nest. *I mean, how far were they going to run with this charade anyway?*

Secretly, my mother sought further counsel regarding my prognosis. She spoke with Dr. Goldblum who did some research. He told her there was still much to learn about the disease as studies had just begun, but my overall health offered considerably more hope than the cases he'd read about.

When push came to shove, I might shove back at my father, but I would ultimately give in to my mother. I was going to airline school, and I think

I was even a little excited to go despite my fear of getting on an airplane. I adapt to changes quickly. In fact, I pride myself on it. I began to rationalize the reasons my mother shared for sending me. My job at the diner had no promise for advancement, I didn't have the grades or the aptitude for the typical classroom, no promise of time for a 2-year degree, but I stopped short of agreeing with my parents in one area; my looks and personality might be good enough to land me a job serving coffee and peanuts on a plane? (*To be fair, my parents were caught somewhere between desperation and denial...dare I say delusion where my looks and personality were concerned*).

Atlantic School of Hartford Airline School was my first home away from home. I had a great time! As a bonus, I graduated near the top of my class! Within a week of my commencement, I had 3 interviews! Then the airlines went on strike. *Ugh!* I returned to my next best field of achievement...fun and trouble, and I made the most of it. My self-assuredness began to grow, too, along with my freedom and it began to not matter so much what other people thought (*who was I kidding?*)!

More importantly, though, at least from my vantage point...I was alive.

Along the way, my diagnosis remained, but my prognosis changed a dozen times. Still, I recklessly celebrated for the next 20 years and accumulated a lot of emotional debt in the process. The people closest to me paid a high price for my unruliness.

The angels continued to work overtime.

TAKE A MOMENT

Loosen your chin strap...

...and allow room for expansion. You may need it.

Take a deep breath.

Exhale and say "So-o-o Hu-u-m-m."
I hope this feels as good to you as it does for me. I learned it in a contemplative mindfulness class. It's Sanskrit, which is a very cool ancient language and it means;

"I am all that!".

On that note, I'd like to insert a disclaimer about my 'that-ness';

Some of my recollections are born of latent possibilities. Some memories are very strong while others have slowly materialized over time; connected to actuality only by process of elimination and/or whatever I believe to be most credible. Hence, my conclusions contain a pinch of conjecture, an ounce of circumstantial evidence and a cup of shallow assurance. Some events are a result of my desperate need to come up with a reasonable explanation. The older I get, it seems, the more the details alter in meaning, which I probably inherited from my grandfather.

Grandpa 'Bud' Tracy was among the greatest storytellers I've ever known, a round and lovable (not too close) musician, comedian and troublemaker who made the most out of the scarcest of visits. He could tell the same story over and again, always with a surprise new ending.

I've struggled with ways to verbalize it, but I have always held a quiet confidence in with the Universe, nevertheless. It does not rely on wishful thinking or witchery. It is real to me and I don't feel the need to apologize for it. My faith keeps me from sinking. Like Einstein's gravitatic theory, it is not something I see or understand; yet somehow feel it to be true. The existence of God is not a product of what I was taught in Sunday School, though. God had my back even before children's church had my attention. The proof is in the pudding, and I am unyielding in my stance until someone sticks a spoon in it. I continue to grow. I probably do not see God in the same manner everyone does, nor am I sure I'm supposed to. What I do know is the believing happened before my remembering began. I am a part of all that is.

I believe in angels, both in spiritual and human likeness. I believe in the power that transcends absence.

My only testimony is this case in point: I am too clumsy a mortal to have gotten this far without some divine intervention.

The Universe offers me a lot of choices and I like to think of myself as someone who takes advantage of her options...and often. I am human, and according to the purveyors of the bold and powerful Omnipotent, I am destined to live out my time here on earth, the result of a fine print agreement I opted for before my enlistment formally began. On the metaphysical plane, I might be a little more practiced than the average human, but you are not average by any means (I've already picked up on that). I am reflective and intuitive, though I refrain from honing any psychic abilities--I rather prefer to be surprised. I consider myself empathic which is just a word suggesting I pick up on the mood when I enter a room, innately zero in on someone's state of mind, then jump into action with compassion and understanding (or run the other way, depending upon my ability to address and manage the situation).

Balance is my goal. Yours too!

See! I am intuitive...and wise!

CHAPTER 5

The Atlantic School of Hartford...

...taught me less about the airline industry and more about life outside of my little neighborhood at home. It wasn't a large school, perhaps 100 students. We lived in furnished dormitories near Farmington Avenue, not very far from Mark Twain's Hartford Home and Museum. It was a beautiful city by all accounts, but I had no car and I didn't see as much downtown as I wanted. Besides the transportation issue, time was somewhat limited as we were assigned a rather rigorous class schedule. We had very pleasant house parents with thick German accents who watched over our comings and goings, insisting on weekly apartment inspections. There were rules for living the campus life; cleanliness, curfew, order. I was pretty good with the first of the three.

And, there was softball. My life was complete. I played pick-up ball in the spring league of a women's slo-pitch in West Hartford. I pitched and caught a little when needed, but my position as shortstop was sealed after one practice. I had a strong arm and was equally impressive with a bat. I was not built for speed, however; the ability to knock the ball wherever there was an opening was a by-product of my inability to outrun a fielder's throw. My time on the field was somewhat hindered by a need to study and a rather active party schedule. Truth be told, I'd rather have played than party, but I was easily persuaded.

I found friendship with one young lady who was about four years my senior. Karen was a fire ball of promiscuity and self-assurance, both a little out of my comfort zone. She commanded attention and received it without deliberation. She took me under her wing, kind of like an apprentice. Everyone respected her (maybe even feared her) and she had quite the audience. She was bisexual, but not openly. I was naïve. In one very enlightening and life-defining moment, I learned more about myself than I bargained for. Though outwardly undaunted by the actions of my classmates, in my own head I was a nervous and curious introvert who just wanted to be liked. Life was moving faster than it did in my West Virginia surroundings, but I had a firm hold on the tail of it. I enjoyed myself thoroughly, attributing my behavior there to another phase for coming of age...and tequila...I blamed tequila, too.

I wasn't the youngest in the class, but not far from it. Like Karen, most of the students were in their early to mid-twenties. I had celebrated my eighteenth birthday the previous fall. Even now, I smile and grimace at the youngster I was. I was plain in appearance, and kind of a goofball. Karen said people liked me because of my kind and non-judgmental nature. This I can attest to, largely a product of my upbringing. Another classmate, whom we affectionately called 'Skeeter', told me I was an old soul (I didn't have a clue what that meant, but I smiled and said 'thank you' anyway). No help was needed for finding trouble, certainly, as I was no saint, but my new friends were always including me in the impressive mischief they designed, partying and other orneriness. Inclusiveness is what I craved, I guess, and my busy schedule offered plenty of opportunities to satisfy those cravings.

I wasn't bad, but my naivete' vaulted me into a few unladylike enterprises, surprising me and everyone else. Still, I recovered nicely. It seemed it was just my time to be noticed. I was a long way from Weirton, W.Va. I had no close friends back home and basked in the raucousness of college life. My allegiance to Karen seemed to propel me into the 'most popular' category but being with her on any level just felt good.

50

I scored well in all classes but for 'Beauty and Charm.' Had I not been able to rely heavily on my paper test scores, I'd have failed the subject miserably. I am still unable to balance a book on my head and gracefully walk twenty feet.

I was given a monthly stipend as part of my loan arrangement (it never lasted more than 48 hours), and I was introduced to marijuana and an over-the-counter caffeine pill, gleefully endorsed by the sorority of procrastination for which I'd become a member. My innate aptitude for putting things off was all the eligibility I needed. It worked well, right up until the unforgiving headache I got for lack of sleep every Friday. *(My entire typing class shared a box of them for a test. Overall speed-typing scores were never higher! You may have already guessed but the dorms were very quiet that evening).* This high-octane caffeine tablet is still available and harmless when taken as directed. There was tequila, too. Painful. There were no directions on a tequila bottle, and I still walk with my head lowered when I pass the liquor aisle in the grocery store.

I survived. Hence, a little more testimony for God's presence...and patience. If you're thinking it just isn't fair for me to have had all these chances, I won't argue, but let me be forthcoming...there is a certain amount of retribution required, and if you think banks came up with the idea for charging interest, you're mistaken. I ran from paying penance, but it would someday catch up with me, interest accrued. I am still making arrangements with the Universe in lieu of past due accounts for bad behavior.

When I graduated Airline School, I returned home, but I was different. I wasn't the innocent, eyes-with-wonder, 'barely a child' daughter my parents put on a plane to Hartford. Depending on the day, I could be sullen or high-spirited, sweet or mean...and I didn't bother to mask my feelings. My mother was delighted to see me, but within a few days, it was clear to both of us I no longer belonged there. I was unrecognizable to her; she seemed different to me. The gap between us was wider than before I left. My siblings had survived just fine without me and the few friends I had were married or gone. Momma offered to let me live with her, but Mom made it clear though she wished I'd stay close, this would only put a wedge in their relationship.

After my short visit home, I moved to Washington D.C. with Karen, a mutual friend, and Karen's sister, also a classmate at Airline School. Finding a job was easy (evidently, I interviewed well) but keeping a job was not one of my strengths. I worked as a receptionist in a law office, then a clerk in an insurance office and a key punch operator for the Daughters of the American Revolution. Sounds impressive, but I didn't last more than a couple of months with any position. My roommates were growing weary of my inability to keep up with my share of the rent and though Karen tried earnestly to keep me in line and steer me in the right direction, I was asked to leave. I returned home, against my own better judgement (though, obviously, I was not worthy of owning one). Once again, I outwore my welcome.

Karen and I stayed in touch. Within a few months, she called to say she thought I should return to try out for a new semi-pro women's softball league based in Chevy Chase, Md. I had no idea there was such a thing. I went, made first team, and got another job at a little hospital in Alexandria Va., not far from the house I shared with 6 other women...it took three buses and over an hour to get me to practice when I couldn't hitch a ride with Karen.

I never missed softball practice and was rarely home, spending most of my free time with Karen and her new 'friend'. I fractured my left hand, the result of a night club fight (not mine...I was collateral damage), and if I was to start the first game, I would need to find a way to get the cast off. Against the advice of the doctor, I did. The coach was quite enamored with my ball-playing skills, but I think he was a bit jealous, too. My first practice after the incident, glove in hand, I've never had a ball thrown so hard at me. I screamed in agony. Karen witnessed the event and ran at this giant of a man, throwing herself on his back and pounding him on his head. The bench cleared and there was an 'in-house' brawl, of sorts. He apologized, I wrapped my hand for the first game, and we won, thanks to a late rally.

I've never been able to fully ascertain the definition for semi-pro ball. We received some minimal income from our sponsor depending on paid attendance (which was sparse) and free drinks after every win, which seemed to be the greater incentive.

I played a total of 5 or 6 games, and then fate opened another door and shoved me through. The house I was living in burned down and I was a girl without a place to stay. I had no clothes, no money, no job, no car, no fielder's mitt...returning home was not an option, and Karen's relationship with another companion was in enough jeopardy, I didn't have the nerve to ask for her help again.

In this instance, and in a host of others, 'fate' may be referenced as a somewhat agitated Universe.

I called my birth father.

CHAPTER 6

Clayton Dewey Gray, *aka* Jerry...

...was a little taken aback by my out-of-the-blue call, but happily arranged for my airfare to New Hampshire where he resided with his common law wife, Lin. I hoped he would send me some money, but his concern for my recklessness was warranted. The relationship between my two new house parents was considered a little weird, I guessed, but I had no problem with it. Together nearly twenty years, they began their courtship when she was just fifteen (my birth father would have been chasing thirty), but the age difference was of little consequence to me. Besides, her family was quite pleased, and as it has often applied with me, the judgments I've held with the behaviors of other people are twofold;

1) Live and let live
2) People in glass houses shouldn't throw stones.

Lin was nice to me from the start. I did have a sense she felt a little left out and I did my best to pal up to her. It wasn't hard. She was personable enough, very much the wife to him that I couldn't picture my Mother being. It was hard not to make comparisons, though I was smart enough to keep them to myself. After all, I was rather practiced in keeping my feelings to myself.

I was also running out of places to live.

They did not have any children. They did have a lot of secrets. Evidently, I'd been one of them. Awkward.

After some explanation and a host of introductions, I became part of the Gray family in North Woodstock, New Hampshire. I was not it the city anymore, but it worked much to my liking. A town lost in time, it felt oddly familiar, but I'd not been part of this world before. Everything projected an older quality. Newly purchased cars and trucks were mostly used. Men gathered in the town square every morning to share the local news and reminisce of days gone by. The town's general store sold fresh eggs and meats (not old, of course). They also served bologna sandwiches, Vermont cheese, hot dogs and a bitter soft drink called Moxie. There was a line of buckets on the floor filled with penny nails in various sizes. These were weighed on the same archaic looking scales as the lunchmeat.

Each day began at 4:30 a.m. and there were always a variety of chores to be started. Six meals were served per day and I loved awakening each morning to largely untamed and picturesque surroundings; White Mountains, Lost River Gorge, the Pemigewasset River, and the Old Man in the Mountain. All were a quick jaunt from our location, but the Lost River was, until we moved, quite literally the backdrop to the land his family owned. The smell of freshly baked ham, bob-house toast and eggs fried in bacon grease were equally appealing for my early morning wake-up.

Jerry, the character starring in many of my childhood daydreams, was much different than the high school picture in my mother's yearbook. His name was also different. Time hadn't been as kind to him as it had my mother. He looked older than his age. There was little to connect him to the handsome high school football star he once was. Quite the contrary, he was shorter and rounder than me, a very simplistic man, he wore the same style of shirt and slacks every day, the waist of which gripped tightly underneath a large bulge of a belly. Everyone knew him as Clay-tee, and he was generally soft-spoken and well-liked. True to his origins, he spoke with a thick New England accent and never left the house without his Avery Brothers hat. He'd been employed as a bulldozer operator for the larger part of his life there, but he proudly called himself a 'pusha' (New England for pusher) which just meant he pushed dirt. Explanations notwithstanding, he seemed proud to have me there, and I was happy for a fresh start. He rather liked the tomboy in me and showed some encouragement by providing everything I could possibly desire to add to the wholesomeness of my new surroundings. We spent many an evening getting to know each other. We went hunting, fishing, camping, snowmobiling and eating, New Hampshire style. We baled hay, chopped firewood, and made homemade root beer in the basement.

He took me on a celebratory snipe hunt (evidently a ritual for newcomers). I learned how to carve and decoratively burn wood, bake beans in a hole dug in the earth, and gut the occasional German Brown trout. There was no baseball, but he put up a basketball hoop under the giant elm and pine trees surrounding the driveway cul-de-sac so that I could exercise my need for being part of the outdoors without being in the direct sun.

Terry's short life had been the topic for many of our heart-to-heart conversations. It was clear to me Clay-tee still mourned his loss but seemed more open to talking about the tragedy than my mother. I never shared my thoughts for the kind of relationship my brother and I shared because I worried people would think me crazy. Though my birth father and I would later be unable to hurdle the irreconcilable terms between us, the details about my original family and its demise both aroused and tamed my long-held curiosities.

Mom and Jerry (as she called him) had been high school sweethearts. They married after graduation and lived in a small trailer park across the Ohio River in a tiny riverside neighborhood call the Pottery Edition. They were happy but he wanted to move closer to his roots in New England. Initially, she was okay with the idea.

May 5,1953: Terry was just shy of three years old when he wandered away from his neighbor's yard, fell into a ravine and died. Both of my parents were devastated but as time wore on, Jerry needed to let go of the heartbreak and move on. Mom struggled for the same and was subsequently pushed further into despair. They were young and emotionally spent. They fought. They tried and then they didn't. They were tired. He left. As stories and their two sides often go, the details described by each for the events leading up to his departure vary a good deal. As for why he didn't try to contact me? Perhaps, he was sincere when he said he felt it too hard on a child to go back and forth between parents. What it really did (in my mind) was put all the pressure on Mom to answer questions and take on the role of two people. In my quietly held opinion, Mom suffered for the added stress. In the end and to this day, what mattered was those he left behind, Mom and me (flawed as our relationship may have been), and all who traveled with us.

I acquired my first job in New Hampshire as a produce clerk at the IGA supermarket and the second at Fantasy Land, a zoo attraction featuring, among others, an adorable pair of Gibbon Apes, an ornery guerilla named Joe, wolves, giraffes, some wild cats, etc. In hindsight, this was one of my lifelong favorites, providing me outdoors with shade from accompanying Green Ash and Sassafras trees, hidden away from the hustle and bustle of my otherwise crazy and disheveled life. The pay was minimal, but the rewards were many; nurturing and medicinal. I felt safe and loved. The animals reacted to me with an unparalleled measure of introspection and compassion through mutual trust and understanding. It was as if they knew me. For all the visitors and staff that passed by their enclosures, they seemed appreciative of my daily visits. They tapped into a goodness I'd nearly lost through foolishness. They nudged me lovingly with their snouts. In just the right doses, I was awarded contact with all of those creatures of God, as well as the environment; the combination conveying a sense of concord I hadn't experienced before.

The surroundings were liberating and humbling. I spent my breaks walking through the complex, always with a feeling of peace. It was an exhilarating experience for my body, my mind and my soul. I experienced a shift towards a personal enlightenment, but I didn't have a name for it. I recall the feeling of being at the center of the Universe. A collection of these tiny increments let me experience what I believed to be my first genuine spiritual revelation on the grounds of the Fantasy Land compound, ironic as the name implies. I felt as close to 'whole' as I could ever remember. I talked with Terry during these sublime moments. He shared the entire journey with me.

At times, Terry spoke to me. Never in a 'little boy' voice and always with a big brother tone, he had the ability to guide my conscience. I had the audacity to argue with him at times, but in the mirror of my life, he was always right. He seemed always to have a firm grip on me, even when the lights dimmed. Once the smoke settled, he pulled me from the ashes. He stood by me. Perhaps our situation wasn't ideal, and it surely wasn't typical, but for never having met him in the flesh, the impact he had on me was paramount.

As for the XP treatments, a specialist at Dartmouth's Rose Hitchcock Cancer Center took on my case. I was given Efudex (acid) in a stronger dose to apply to my face twice a day for three weeks. This would help to highlight cancerous areas of sun-damaged skin. The affected areas weren't always easy to see, and when they did rise to the surface, it was just harder to deal with them. Two weeks into the process and my face looked like a ball of red hamburger meat. I went to bed one night with a slightly red and irritated face and awakened the next day with a very red and bleeding surface. I was admitted to the Dartmouth-Hitchcock Cancer

Center with a nasty infection that had quickly navigated its way through the rest of my body. I was septic and near death. Apparently, and to add to my dilemma, I was allergic to the cortisone cream I applied post-Efudex.

Throughout the XP ordeal, I'd been prescribed various creams and solutions to detect and eliminate cancer cells before they became visible on my skin. Efudex (fluorouracil 5-FU) is a very strong topical chemo...acid-like. Its purpose is to kill the cancerous cells on the skin and leave the good cells alone by attacking DNA production. I have had both success and misery with these ointments, and as recent as this year have been prescribed them again. The cream is potent and harsh, but difficult situations require difficult measures. To be fair, I am thin-skinned and very sensitive to many direct applications. I've managed to bleed in the shower if the force of the water is too harsh.

Perhaps it was my offhanded attitude or maybe this was just part of the hospital's protocol, but I was assigned a psychiatrist. He asked me questions like 'what were my dreams before the diagnosis', and 'how was I coping'. Whatever his intent, he obviously never got to the crux of why I wasn't scared or angry or upset. Maybe I wasn't taking it seriously enough, but I'd internally posed the questions time and again, and for the most intense of these interrogations; "How do you view death?", my answer was quite practical, "I believe if my brother could do it, I can to." Perhaps I didn't fully realize the scope of what was happening, perhaps I was a smartass. Again, though, not to be redundant in testimony, I felt safe: I was going to be okay...whatever I was going through, I would be okay, *even if I wasn't.*

To lend a little more insight into my air of confidence, I was a patient of Dr. Clendenning, a world-renowned dermatologist who personally knew Dr. James Cleaver, the leading XP and DNA research scientist who'd been instrumental in discovering the mutation and detecting a link for DNA disorders such as mine. XP was (and still is) quite rare. In the United States, its odds are a million to one. At this time in my life, most dermatologists and other doctors hadn't even heard the term. Yet, in every part of the country I lived, I encountered an informed physician. Highly unlikely for someone else, perhaps, but completely normal for this girl from small town WV. Did I mention I believe in angels?

Bonus: Dr. Clendenning was also the first to explain my original prognosis for an early demise to be premature. "Take care of yourself" he said, "and you could live to be as old as me." He looked to be around 50 years old. I didn't believe him, but even if I had, death was an arrangement I'd come to terms with by this time. I simply wasn't afraid of it.

Discharged and home, life was beginning to settle for me. I worked evenings and weekends for a wonderfully cantankerous woman in the produce section of the grocery store. We called her Poppy, "after the flower" she'd say a bit defensively. She didn't have the title of store manager but there was no doubt she was in charge. She knew Clay-tee (everybody did) and she was aware of the stories surrounding him. Her husband of forty odd years had passed away. She lived alone but for Izzy's 'after death' visits and I loved hearing 'their' stories. We loved trading the tales of life in two worlds. In her firm but simplistic way, she enjoyed sharing the same conviction for spiritual awareness other people were quick to denounce.

I purchased my first car with Clay-tee's help; a 1973 used AMC Gremlin I named Gert, and because I was living rent-free there, I was well on my way to having enough money to put down on a new car. I was taking correspondence classes from ICS (a mail order school, no less) for accounting (it bemuses me to this day) and to add to my good fortune, I was the central focus of a new family. It was an oddly satisfying time in my life.

Except for one inescapable fact.

I missed my 'real' family, and they had no idea where I was. I no longer felt self-righteous. I felt selfish. Mom was certainly worried, and my siblings were undoubtedly caught up in the drama surrounding my absence even if it wasn't talked about (which, knowing my mother, it wasn't). I needed to see all of my brothers and sisters, my Mom and Dad, and Momma, too. It was late summer and after much deliberation, I put aside my anxiousness for how I might be received. I called Momma to wish her 'Happy Birthday'. She seemed unphased by my call, almost as though she was expecting it. We talked for about ten minutes when I asked her what she wanted for her birthday.

"I only want one thing. I want you to call your mother."

I wasn't surprised. I was relieved.

Much as my pride worked to dismiss and forgive my irresponsible behavior, I'd carried the regret of the last words I selfishly said to my mother; "You never really loved me anyway, Mom. I've always just been in the way, and you know it."

Years later, I remember the look of hurt on her face.

I cringe.

CHAPTER 7

I left New Hampshire...

...on fairly good terms, but, full disclosure, Clay-tee wasn't entirely happy about it. Still, he didn't put up much of a fight. Fantasy Land had closed for the season, and when the seasons changed, the layoffs began. IGA could only offer me a few hours a week, so my visit home was well-planned...or so it seemed. Initially I thought I'd work in Weirton somewhere part-time for the winter, then return to New Hampshire, but my mother was visibly upset when I exclaimed my stay at home to be temporary. With little hesitation, I altered my original plan and decided to get a full-time job and return to WV to reside. I put my application in at the steel mill.

At this juncture, my birth father was more than a little upset. I returned to NH to pick up the rest of my things and we barely spoke. He believed I was making a big mistake. He may have been right, but as always, I felt as though I was being pulled in the direction of home. I had no crystal ball to see how things might have been once there. I would wait a long time for my life to unfold favorably, but it did, indeed, do just that.

I have often wondered how things may have gone had I stayed, but I missed my family, and though things didn't go as well as I might have hoped, I wouldn't regret the move. They say one can never return home again, but what they really mean is one should never return home again. I wound up at home time and time again...with the same results. I failed, quite miserably, at being a young adult in good standing with my family. At times I tried hard and I failed. Sometimes when I tried it was out of desperation and my timing was off, or my goals were no more than wishful thoughts. It seemed I was always searching for who I was supposed to be. *Who was I?* For all intents and purposes, I was an undisciplined and irresponsible young adult, recklessly engaged in behaving badly...drugs and alcohol, lies and pretense. I partied...hard. I hid the truth so well I couldn't find it myself. I gave allegiance to recklessness and shunned the efforts of everyone who tried to help me. I was sure things would turn around for me as they did when I was in NH. I came home to my mother, and we were strangers. She hadn't changed. It was me. I waited for the bounce; that dramatic shift in consciousness when the Universe would strengthen my spirit. My childhood may have been robbed of innocence, but as an adult I was the victim of my own bad judgement and behavior. I was serving my soul to old demons masquerading as new opportunities.

I took a job as laborer for Weirton Steel within a couple weeks of my return, but just shy of me working long enough to receive unemployment benefits, I was laid off...along with several hundred others. Hoping they'd soon call me back to work I took a menial job working for my brother Randy. He owned a gas station in town, needed some cheap help, and I needed money. He could only pay me $1/hour, but I found the work to be both easy and boring. More importantly, though, I had a reason to get up and go each day. The tediousness for pumping gas and washing car windows turned out to be only a little less challenging than playing clarinet in the band, but I loved surprising people with my presence. Girls rarely pumped gas back then.

Working for Randy had its rewards, though they weren't in the form of pay. Randy and I had never been particularly close (or alike for that matter) but we held a sort of bond I wouldn't find with my other siblings...not a better one, but an exclusive one. We were of the same biological parents and this strangely connected us in an annoying and timeless way, but just about the only thing we shared a passion for was playing ball. He was a good player, but I often felt as though he had to try harder to shine. He was kind of small in stature, dare I say a lot tamer and quieter than me. As children, we fought often and aside from sports, we went in different directions entirely.

When I worked for Randy, he was a young entrepreneur, a better than average mechanic, married and a new father. I understood he couldn't afford to pay me so much, and I was just tickled to be there. I pumped gas and washed windshields and occasionally tackled something on a bigger scale, but none so big as the day he asked me to change the oil on a shiny new 1977 cherry red Chevy pick-up truck. I was a little surprised by his request since I'd never changed oil before. The guy was a friend of his; Gregg Jones.

In Randy's defense, he did explain the process to me. I did nod in the affirmative when he said "Simple, right?"

Actually, it went quite smoothly.

Until Mr. Jones' truck reached the top of Cove Hill. Suddenly, blue smoke was frantic to escape from under the hood. His oil gage said EMPTY.

Meanwhile, back at the station...

I swept up the garage area and ran across a small black item resembling a plug of some kind.

Gregg Jones and I...

...were married and expecting our first child within a year. It was an ill-advised union and we both knew it. Wedded bliss is hard to materialize when neither spouse is up to the challenge, but opportunities for success did appear from time to time...three more children would follow.   All healthy and beautiful and smart....and precious. God delivered more than enough, but we squandered away any trust or good feelings one of us might have had for the other. Acting like adults might have been a start, but we were aimless, one of the few things we had in common and perhaps the very reason we were drawn to each other. Neither of us dwelled on the details, barely recognized them as a matter of fact, and we didn't have a plan. I was silly enough to believe I could confide in him my fears about my sexuality. *Very bad idea.* We were hopelessly immature and completely disconnected, and Terry stepped aside from me completely...my other brothers did, too...they all loved Gregg.

I worked throughout our marriage at menial jobs and while the pay helped, it did little to support our growing family. We had no health coverage, and my treatments never fell at a good time. I was hopelessly delinquent in keeping up with appointments, but I had to work, and surgeries cut into our income. Gregg found the only incentive to his liking to be at the racetrack, gambling. His efforts proved in vain, and in fact, only leant to our growing financial problems. The ponies were hardly sustainable for daily sundries and necessities. I was employed as a cook at four different homestyle restaurants on either the first or third shifts (sometimes both) during my 13 years with Greg...a clerk at the 7Eleven, and a laborer for a local industrial stamping plant. In our first year together, I was finally re-called to work in the mill but as luck would have it, I was pregnant and would not pass the physical. At the time, women didn't have considerations for pregnancy or mothering. In fact, one of the questions during interviews for ladies of child-bearing age was "Do you plan on having children?"

I continued to play ball throughout my twenties. Other than the time spent with my children, it was among my only remaining joys. Yes, I was outside in the sun, and yes, I knew it was harmful, but I just couldn't give it up. I did my best to manage the two worlds. I wore sunscreen and tried to remember to reapply it. I wore dark glasses to protect my eyes. I wore the typical ball cap, and while my hair wasn't very long, it sufficed to fall over my ears and act as a shield. Mercifully, mid-day games were rare, and when I wasn't on the field, I kept myself in the shade. At the time, I was not fully on board with what my doctors were saying about my condition. I was told, for example, the effects of the ultraviolet rays would take fifteen years to materialize. Yet, I was in my twenties and my skin was remarkably healthy with only minor blemishes. Fifteen to twenty years would have found me in the sun all day...always playing ball. I had not yet been told that U/V rays reflect, the shade offering little resilience. My body was in excellent shape, though, and for the horrors associated with XP, I'd only experienced one other noticeable breakdown in my anatomy, and it had nothing to do with the sun, and everything to do with the hazards of playing outdoor sports. I turned on second base for a double play to first and tore cartilage and ligaments in my knee. I had no insurance (again) and lived and worked through the pain for the better part of the years remaining. I also continued to play ball.

We rented a trailer in a couple parks outside of town and were asked to leave for not paying rent on time...twice. With Gregg's parents' help, we bought our own trailer and moved into another park. Gregg finally took a trucking job for a steel hauler but was quickly laid off. For the first few years, it was on again and then off. Then he was in an accident. As far as I could tell, his injuries were not remotely serious, but he never received another paycheck. His parents bought us a home in the same neighborhood they resided, and as happy as we were to be out of a trailer park, it only compounded our problems.

Momma continued to be my salvation when I needed an ear to bend or a shoulder to cry on. She was starting to show her age a bit, but she still worked and always found time for me. I looked forward to weekly trips to town to meet her for coffee, biscuits and conversation. She took ill in her mid-70s. The diagnosis; lung cancer, a sadly common diagnosis for residents of the graphite laden mill town we lived in. She was gone within a year, and to date, these were among the toughest days I'd endured. With my longest friend and confidant gone, my life was in a shamble; my faith was waning, my self-esteem did not exist. I desperately wanted to give up. Within a month of her funeral, weeks into what could be compared to a suicidal slide, she came to me in a dream.

Momma sat in a high back chair center of an otherwise empty room. Terry, dressed in the clothes he wore in his portrait, appeared from the right (her left) and climbed upon her lap. They said nothing but their expressions spoke loudly. From a place of love and forgiveness, they encouraged me. I can't say why I knew this to be a message, but immediately I felt it to be a personal directive. I awakened, shaken and afraid, springing from bed and suddenly worried for my children, I found them all to be as I'd left them, safely and quietly in their beds. As I lay down to resume sleep, the meaning became clear; I was not focusing on the most important of all God's gifts, and for their sake, I needed to move on. I remember laying on my back and staring at the ceiling, my arms crossed over my chest, hugging myself. Tears formed in my eyes and silently streamed down my cheeks. I mouthed "I'll try".

The following day, and perhaps the first time in the decade I'd known my husband, we talked. We proceeded clumsily and a bit cynically, at first, but it was a start. For a brief time, it looked like we could save our little family...and ourselves. The Universe threw us another curve, though, and we were thrust back into gracelessness. Over, and over again, we returned to the safety of being too afraid to move the feet of our souls.

My father (Dave) died unexpectedly. He was 51 years old. He'd been complaining of pressure in his chest and my mother suggested he see the doctor. The doctor ran a stress test with inconclusive results, then issued a request for more tests. Near the end of a routine heart catherization, my father had a massive heart attack.

I was watching a tiny television with my mother that morning in a crowded waiting room at Weirton Medical Center. "Code Blue" echoed over the loudspeaker, and I was surprised by my mother's declaration. "It's your Dad" she said. "It's Dave."

I looked at her in complete puzzlement. "No, Mom" I said, doing my best to quell her anxiety (this wasn't like her at all). I spread my arms as to strengthen my argument with the large number of people who might have reasons to feel the same way. "Why would you say that?" I asked.

She did not look at me. She looked straight ahead. Her lips quivered and she straightened her back. She felt it. I looked around the crowded room, and there wasn't another soul who appeared to panic.

"I know" she said softly, "I just know."

She was right.

In my desperate effort to make sense of the tragedy, I rearranged my focus once again. It seemed, though, no matter my intention, I couldn't console her. It was the same as it had always been. My siblings seemed to have no trouble saying what she needed or wanted to hear. The words escaping me, however, sounded stale and ineffective. I wanted to hold her. I couldn't. It seemed so effortless for my siblings to engage, but I felt pushed back from her again and again.

"We're going to be okay, Mom" I said as we left the hospital after his death.

She looked at me with a face of stone. "What other choice do we have, Debby?"

She fell into Gregg's arms and sobbed.

A number of months passed, and healing was slow but steady. My mother had lost so much, but her strength and undeniable grace always kept the rest of us moving forward. She kept herself busy, giving all of herself to the rest of us, her skill as an optician, and taking care of the great big house once filled with so much promise. I acquired a position (with my mother's help) as receptionist for a young optometrist in the vision center for which she worked. I had big shoes to fill, but she was very excited to teach me all about opticianry. She drove out of her way countless times to get me to and from work. A new bond began to fill the cracks in our relationship.

My self-confidence slowly grew and so did my zeal for learning a trade. I studied for the Optical Board Exam (A.B.O.C.), took a position as Optician (apprentice) with a national chain, then passed the test...barely. Still, it was quite a feat and I knew it. Half of the applicants failed on their first attempt. It seemed as though my life had new meaning; I'd found my niche. I was hired by the national chain who paid for my Board Exam. Things were looking up for me, professionally, but my relationship with Gregg was faltering and I couldn't talk to my mother about it. Momma was gone.

Within a few short weeks of getting my new job, Gregg's father was diagnosed with lung cancer. He fought hard but passed away the following April. We were both devastated. These tragedies didn't pull us together. Rather, they drove the wedge deeper. We were both in mourning. Like two children, we fought through our grief by hurling insensitivities at each other. We argued hard and often, mired in misery and selfishness, displaying only spurts of tolerance for one another. At times we were the best of friends, sharing our grievances for the unfairness of our pathetic predicaments, but more often, we held each other accountable.

Time went slowly for a while. Gregg and our friend Tony went to Maine on a hunting trip. While there, he stopped to see Clay-tee. Gregg called to tell me my birth father died of cardiac arrest a few months earlier. I wasn't notified because Lin believed it unnecessary to call me with the news. Somehow, I understood this.

The relationship with my birth father and his wife soured almost as quickly as I moved back home. He wrote. I wrote. We talked a couple of times, and even had a lengthy stay there in the winter. It was at this time a problem occurred; an accusation, really. I was in good standing with a place I'd worked and managed to get Lin's sister-in-law a job. She was very appreciative, but a rumor evolved with her working there, and I was put squarely in the middle. I tried to explain the circumstances to Lin and Clay-tee but before I had the chance, I was attacked for 'my' callousness. I was deeply hurt and offended. Gregg and I packed up our family, almost immediately, and there was little communication to follow.

Time and circumstance interfered to some extent, but the truth had settled long before then. I could have gone through my life never knowing him at all, so there was that. I won't say I mourned his loss. I'm not sure how I felt. There had been so many disappointments to this point in my life. He had been one of them, just as sure as I had been to him. I learned to accept responsibility for all of it. The delayed, back-door announcement of his death served to remind me of my place, and there was only so much I could allow myself to suffer for it again.

There were times such as these that Gregg was a rock for me. He told Clay-tee's wife he thought it unfair not to notify me. Perhaps it was Clay-tee's wishes, but Gregg softly told me "Debby, being upset with him is as wrong as he was not to respond to your last letter (months before he died). You can't possibly know how he felt. You were his daughter, and some people just aren't capable of loving their kids." Gregg, nor I, were horribly bad people, but we brought out the best (our kids) and worst (our insecurities) in each other. We were at odds in nearly every area of our relationship, but at times, hope shined bright.

When I wasn't working, I was mostly visiting with my mother. For a while, it felt as though we were breaking through the thick but invisible wall that separated us. We bonded, somewhat, but it never gelled. I complained about my marriage often, but she took a stand against interfering and though it meant she wouldn't take sides, (my side), I understood it. She seemed to accept Gregg as another one of her kids, and though he and I were largely at odds with one another, I respected her stance.

Ultimately, Gregg and I both wanted more, and we both deserved more than what each of us could provide the other. I wanted a husband I could trust; he couldn't be trusted, and I couldn't be trusted either. He would stand accused of some things hard to deny, but I lied to protect him. It would be a dozen years before I gave up on our marriage, because I believed he loved me to a degree I might never be loved again...something about him was good enough to hold onto. If only I could change him, it might change things for us...it might even change me!

 Meanwhile, skin cancer began to introduce me to consequences for 'sun carelessness'. Stress, I was told, exacerbated any weakness or condition, too, supplying a feeding ground for cancer cells. I was in no short supply. Pittsburgh, specifically the University of Pittsburgh, had long been a 'go to' for me, a quick thirty minutes from my home. The surgeon's office was located on the Southside of the Steel City in a medical complex. Most procedures were of the out-patient variety. I was not surprised to learn I needed 16 biopsies, a personal record for me…one I'm not particularly fond of.

Enter the angels once again.

There are three types of skin cancer. The most common and least threatening are basal cell carcinomas. Squamous cell is a bit trickier and melanomas, the scariest and deadliest. We were all stunned to find all but one were basal cell carcinomas; the other, squamous. They all needed to be removed, though, and after just a week's wait, I was recuperating nicely. I continued to work, spending less time on the front end of the store and more in the lab, preferring to heal without commentary. As manager of the vision center, I could schedule myself in the lens finishing area or just hang out with the massive stacks of paperwork in my office. *Anything, really, just to avoid; "Oh my, I hate to ask, but what happened to your face? "Oh, dear, did you fall down the stairs?" "I'm guessing you were in an accident. Did your face hit the windshield?" "Were you burned in a fire?"* (I've heard them all).

As it often occurred before the healing was through, two more places appeared; one on my lower left eyelid and the other on my right eyebrow. Both would require Mohs, (a procedure that works to save as much skin as possible), but the one on my eyelid was large enough it needed closed by a plastic surgeon. Because the healing required a graft, my upper left lid was sewn to my left cheek for three weeks to allow for the cleanest and safest way to 'take'. This time, I would not be able to work. The dust from the lab might have caused infections to hinder proper healing. My surgeon recommended I take a month off. I was at least two weeks without pay which we couldn't afford.

There were some situations without possibility of change, however, and Gregg, nor I, had no control of them. I couldn't hold a job, mostly a by-product of my condition. Gregg wouldn't get a job, mostly because he didn't try. I loved to work, though, and I rarely missed an opportunity getting a job I applied for. A better than average worker, and an equally effective leader, people responded well to my efforts. But...open wounds are unattractive and take away from one's performance. For months at a time, I enjoyed the freedom of no apparent health problems, but sooner or later, the consequences of this debilitating condition bled through. Literally. I always needed more time for surgeries and healing than my employers allowed. I often ignored cancerous tumors on my skin just to delay the possibility of being let go. This worked well until the lesions appeared on my face.

The W.Va. Dept. of Rehabilitation offered me a chance to go to college at minimal cost, and I seized the opportunity. I did well, but problems at home were beginning to mount, financially and otherwise. I stopped going to college shy of getting my degree. Still, I landed a job as an optician at another national chain, and within months was promoted to manager. A year later, I found myself in line for another position and one more suitable for my skin limitations. I was to be promoted to 'point', a position that steered me away from eye-to-eye contact with the general public and allowed me the space and the time to heal without hurry or judgement. The job paid well but required me to travel at times. I loved the idea.

Gregg did not.

CHAPTER 8

Tension was rising...

...between my husband and me. It rose from the cellar of distrust to the ceiling of contempt. He felt no responsibility for our financial situation and had little sympathy for my restrictions for working outside the home. Our children witnessed some of our childish temper tantrums, but by the grace of God, were spared the worst of them.

Until one early June evening.

I remember the argument well. We went through the ceiling and punctured the proverbial roof.

I'd socked away a little money from my last paycheck to purchase new clothes and to go away for the day with some friends at work. I didn't tell Gregg because I knew there would be resistance. To this point, I'd had little free time to enjoy myself, and most of my business casual wear consisted of hand-me-downs from Gregg's mother. I was grateful for the offer, but I resented dressing like a senior citizen. I was feeling pretty good about myself, had been promoted to 'Point' manager and was well on my way, I thought, to another promotion as Location Setter. I would set up the vision centers at new sites and help staff them. My boss, 'D', was a good-looking young man, smart and stylish. I was trying to gain some notoriety myself and felt the need to dress for success.

Looking for a place to work without windows is difficult, but the optical chain I where I was employed did business in a larger retail facility. The *ability to wear 'normal' clothing was always met with relief. The larger and less stylish portion of my wardrobe (my sun-wear), however, is devoted to keeping me safe. A simple long sleeve blouse can cost $100, long-sleeve t-shirts, $50-$75, none of it covered by medical insurance.*

I took money, planned a day with friends, and bought new clothes. I lied to Gregg and told him I was in a meeting. He didn't buy it; he waited in his car at the bottom of Florence Road for me to turn toward home. Hidden in a shallow turn-off behind some overgrown brush, Gregg peeled out after me and chased me home. It appeared he was trying to run my car off the narrow winding road. My heart raced. My husband was an expert behind the wheel, and I knew that if he wanted to kill me, he could have. Fear took over. My car swerved from left to right on those dark country roads and I pulled into our driveway suddenly aware I'd been holding my breath. I ran into the house. He was right behind me.

He'd caught me in a lie, and was furious because the house payment was due, the phone was going to be turned off and I was 'selfish'. I was fully prepared to engage in an argument, and beyond my wild fright, I was feeling pretty badly about my actions, but the last words he slung at me transformed the quarrel into physical assault. Years of pent up hostility reached an all-time high, and I went berserk, shamelessly throwing things from the counter, pushing and taunting him to hit me. It peaked with an incredulous "Are you kidding me right now?" and quickly vaulted into; "You ungrateful bastard" and within a flash, "Go ahead, big man!" I screamed "Hit me! I dare you!" Even as I admit to this now, it stings. It is not who I am...it is not who I ever was, really. I feel my face flush with disgrace. But on this day all those years ago, I was in such a rage...I pulled my arm back to give myself the force to hit him hard....to hurt him... to make him feel every ounce of my disdain. But as I thrust my arm forward, I saw something flash in my periphery. A light?

Time seemed to unwind in slow motion. Center of the light, just inside the back door stood my oldest daughter, Shelley, shielding her younger siblings from the ugliness she managed to escape too many times over her young life; her hands firmly covering the eyes of her sisters, her little brother tucked between them, his face buried in her side. Shelley stood tall, consumed with fear herself, but brave enough to protect them from what they shouldn't have to see.

My arm jerked to a halt as though someone or something grabbed it. *Terry?* Gregg's arm was positioned to defend himself. I saw the fear in his eyes, too, for the first time. I recoiled, gulped a deep breath and looked at my four beautiful children. My mouth fell open and I saw my image mirrored in their eyes. I was instantly sickened at who I was, who I'd become. I looked back at Gregg. He didn't know what to expect. He slowly lowered his arm. "I can't..." was all I could muster. I quietly pleaded with God to forgive me as I tearfully, shamefully ran out the door.

The scene has played over and over in my mind since, and it never gets easier to watch. It scares me to think what might have happened had Terry or a host of angels not shown up when they did. These mysterious interruptions from the Universe were precisely measured. It wasn't as though I questioned the out-of-the-blue interference, as much as I marveled at the mastery...and the timing. I've nothing to support my belief, but for the fact I am alive to share my story. For the entirety of my life, all my missteps and blunders, stupidity and recklessness, the odds for a catastrophic end held a much greater advantage. Yet...?

For years I put the weight of my relationship woes on Gregg, but in my defense, it would be hard to argue his portrayal as the 'bad guy.' He had built quite the reputation as being a really nice guy you just couldn't trust. He had a gambling addiction and the symptoms were catastrophic. My response wasn't any better. He was in complete control of the money I earned, and complained it wasn't near enough. There was never enough to go around, but he always had money for the ponies. Our troubled marriage was as sure a bet as the horses he gambled on at Mountaineer Park. Our friends and family took sides because that is what friends and family do, I suppose. There shouldn't have been division...there shouldn't have been an 'all or nothing' camp for either of us. We were both wrong. Unable to find the support I needed, I found it difficult to reference Gregg in any good light at all. He responded in kind. Yet, when he and I were together without the traditional pomp and circumstance of whose fault it was, we got along quite well. It was the living together we couldn't manage. *Living with anyone seemed to be a problem for me.*

My youngest sister, Linda, and I have often talked with regard to the fairy tales we believed awaited us when we started our own families. We knew only what we knew from our parents who despite the craziness of a large household never appeared to stumble in their love affair with one another. They certainly didn't have it easy, but they were consistent and balanced like no other couple we'd witnessed. They were united. They were one.

The gut-wrenching decision to leave my husband was that I would be leaving my children, too. I wanted to take them. I kidded myself into thinking the possibility existed, but I could barely afford to get a place of my own, let alone a home suitable for all of us. I cried. I prayed. I promised God I would turn my life around if only He would help me find a way. I talked with Shelley. She cried and begged me not to leave. She was thirteen years old. She needed me more than ever. She was angry with her Dad but felt my departure would only make things worse. Her sadness ran deep...exposing years of false calm. I watched her tell her story and I saw myself. She was the younger version of me; scared and uncertain for the words available to make a difference. I told her I would try to stay, but my words held more regret than resolve. Each of us only wanted to make things better. I was gone in less than two weeks.

The arguing turned violent once again when I went to visit. Gregg chased me from the house in a fit of fury, grabbed a log from our wood pile and threw it at me. He missed. I jumped in my car and raced away, eventually seeking refuge in the home of a friend from work. Lisa and her partner were nice enough to let me stay with them until I could find another place to live, but by virtue of living with a same-sex couple, the speculation started...from others, from a place within myself. To that end, a reckoning was in the making.

Gregg changed his approach and attempted to meet me with understanding. I continued to see our children, but sorely missed my daily routines with them. They struggled to let go with each visit, often pleading with me to come home. I promised I would come for them, but they seemed less than eager to leave their father, their home and their friends. Ultimately, I responded by taking on the bigger role with my employer to travel and set stores. I threw myself into work and distanced myself from almost everyone except my children, but they barely recognized me, and I couldn't bear to look at myself. Within three months, I lost nearly 40 pounds. Looking back, I was devoid of happiness; consumed with fear and self-doubt.

Numb. This is how I would describe myself after separating from my family. And alone. My light was dimming, fading like the sunset before a New Moon. Questions surfaced: What kind of mother leaves her children? Had I carried the same torch as my birth father prophesying me to imitate his actions and abandon my children? Was I punishing him? Or did I secretly blame myself for his departure? Had I sabotaged my life to get back at my mother for not allowing me to fill the void after Terry's death? Was my thinking so twisted, my childish allegiance to Terry so corrupt and selfish that I used it to destroy the lives of anybody foolish enough to love me? What, indeed, was wrong with me, and why couldn't I fix it?

My mother pleaded with me to return to Gregg. In previous years, she had gone deaf with frustration for the constant complaining about my marital problems, either alluding to the difficulties in 'every' marriage or in the many ways I might change his behavior by reacting differently. My mother was subtle, but I understood her words to mean she thought I was being unrealistic. We had both learned to hear the things we didn't say. It would take several months for her to find peace with the situation, at least outwardly so. Still, each time I picked up the kids and went to visit, she asked about Gregg. To be fair, I was conflicted in several areas of my life, and it may have been difficult for her to say anything that didn't touch on a nerve already exposed and sensitive.

To add to my growing list of frustrations, Shelley began to experience trouble at school (most certainly the result of my leaving home), my second child, Jessica, was suffering from some mysterious food allergy, and my baby, Chip (4), broke his collarbone. Twice. Kelsey, just five years old, owning a typical child's growing curiosity, repeatedly begged me for a response I couldn't satisfy. "Why can't you stay here, Mommy? I miss you! Please??" My sister wrote me a discerning letter airing her disappointment for my selfish behavior and the divide between me and everyone was widening. Now it was me growing smaller and disappearing against the horizon.

I was in worse shape, emotionally, than when Momma died. I attempted to 'handle' each situation as it arose, showing false bravado for my tough side, but truth be told I was hardly coping. I was falling apart. I nibbled at popcorn since I lacked any other craving for food. Small growths on my skin began to bleed through my clothes. I suffered one illness after another, probably a result of my body's attempt to warn me I couldn't survive at the pace I was going. I absorbed the disapproving glares and muffled whispers from hand-covered mouths of people I used to call friends. The only place I felt comfortable was in the workplace and on more than one occasion I stayed in the office overnight. I threw myself into one project after another in the lab, and during open hours I was surrounded with support, appreciation, and kudos for a job well done. Work was a safe place for me to shut down and shut out.

Then, something unthinkable happened that threatened the only thread of dignity and purpose left within me.

I needed help. I needed to disappear if I was to survive, and my options to claim my children beforehand required more time, money and planning. The Universe was pushing, and I was pushing back. *Guess who was winning?*

I gave in.

I called an old friend.

CHAPTER 9

It took me a few days...

...and a lot of nerve to locate Karen. I hadn't spoken to her since my last trip to D.C. nearly fifteen years prior. She was living in Harrisburg, Pa., worked for Pennsylvania Blue Shield, and owned a small kiosk at a local antique barn. I'd nearly talked myself out of making the call since her mother didn't seem keen on telling me where to find her, but I was on a slippery slope at work and too desperate not to try. To say I was nervous about our reunion would be an understatement, but there seemed to be nowhere else to turn. I was somewhat surprised for how excited she was to hear from me, and I accepted her invitation to go and visit for a weekend. My mind formed images for how she must have aged, but reality proved them wrong. She had changed little. I had changed much. I knew this in the instant she opened the door to greet me.

"Livingston!" she shouted gleefully. (Karen knew my first name, but I don't remember her ever calling me by anything other than the last name on my birth certificate, and it meant the world to me. Hard to explain, but it always felt good).

"How the hell are ya'!" She grabbed me in a bear hug, a cold bottle of beer in each of her outstretched arms. "Holy Shit!" she said as she pushed back from me. It seemed she was genuinely happy to see me, even if she couldn't believe it. If Shit was indeed Holy, she was more religious than I remembered. She said it again and again as we did a quick 'catch up'. She shook her head and smiled.

We talked for a while, mostly in review of our antics in Hartford. Karen's large brown eyes sparkled with energy and enthusiasm; but for her ornery grin, her single most attractive feature. It felt good to be with someone who had no ill judgement of me...not yet, anyway...the visit, after all, just started. Slowly, intermittently, I inserted details of my sad life into our joyful reunion, poking fun at the unrecognizable person I'd become *'que sera, sera'*. She listened, attentively, but every time I paused and looked her way, a smile stretched from one high cheek bone to the other. "Holy Shit, Livingston, you're here! You're really freaking here!" In these moments, it occurred to me I might have stumbled into something I'd not experienced in a very long time...a feeling of welcome. I was desperate not to screw it up.

She told me she'd been in a couple of relationships but nothing serious. "I ain't found anybody who can put up with my shit, Livingston!"

Yeah, she was probably right.

We never discussed the personal history we shared all those years ago, and I was relieved. I was little more than a child at the time, and she had probably spent some time beating herself up for the part she played in my 'coming of age.'

There was no 'coming out'. It didn't exist outside of the bedroom. For me, it seemed to be more an exploration; or, I was just needy and loved the physical attention. There was never a discussion about it.

I loved her in a very platonic way, at ease discussing my life and my deepest thoughts, receiving no judgement on the turn around. In one very short evening, we picked up as though time was a myth. Karen was the only person in my world with whom I felt so comfortable. Like bathing in warm rushing water, I cleansed my soul in the flow of our mutual caring and understanding. The persistent push by the Universe did not go unnoticed, and with each intervention, I gave a little more of myself to the power of it. In return, God gave me more opportunities for discovery, and a little more room for redemption. I ached for my children, though, and busied my schedule to fill the void of their company.

The weekend went quickly, and she promised to visit me within the month. We went back and forth like this for a while. Questioning my sexual orientation, I eventually asked questions from her I wouldn't ask of anyone else. I lacked trust with men, no doubt due to the abandonment of my father, the assault by my neighbor and the 'less than' feeling of inclusion from the man who raised me, and the experience I had in a heterosexual marriage. Did I hate men? I didn't think so but trusting them was another matter. *Or,* was I looking at it all sideways? Was the inability to bond with my mother the overarching theme in my desire to share my life with a woman? It all mattered to me. I needed to understand why I was different.

"Aw shit, Livingston, do I look like a shrink?" she bellowed (and swore). "If you're looking for freaking absolution, you're talking to the wrong Indian!"

Karen was, in fact, part French Canadian Indian and part German, but looked to me like a full-blooded Cherokee. Karen was extremely proud of her Native American heritage. In addition to her high cheekbones, thick eyebrows and dark brown eyes, she kept her long black hair parted in the middle and draped over each shoulder. She was shorter than me, but I always looked up to her and she walked as though she owned the land beneath her feet. She partied hard, even all these years later, and toyed on occasion with recreational drugs, making no apologies for her behavior while making a point to steer me away from the heavier stuff. She looked out for me, always, even if she had a hard time taking care of herself. If the plan of the Universe was such for me to choose the angels to travel earth with me, I, no doubt, picked her among them.

My mother and I continued to communicate as best we knew how, which wasn't very good at all. So, on a day she asked me to meet her for coffee and a Danish for an unscheduled 'chat', I assumed we would skim over the same topic of my family status and hear all the reasons why she thought I was acting irrationally. I loved being with my mother even in circumstances such as these. Some might think me a glutton for punishment, but my mother possessed a softness and a grace like no other. She just always felt safe even when it was her intent to administer punishment. There were few surprises talking to Mom, and in my current mental and emotional state, I was just happy to join her, regardless of the reason.

She sat nervously across from me at a small, boutique-size table in a little café at the north end of Main Street in town. It was a new, one-room eatery in an old building with a limited but decadent pastry selection. I was unusually nervous; my thoughts, futile and traitorous. I had gone through the same motions over and again, never expecting the result to change in my favor, rather absorbing each blow wielded at me till I couldn't feel them. Numb once more. The past few days were strange; as though I was watching my life instead of living it...dreamlike, detached, a stranger in search of a new identity...or an old one coming back with revenge. I felt a curious pull, as though something was about to happen, but I ignored it, deliberately. I didn't trust it. I was emotionally dazed, mired in the muddy folds of my mind, stubborn to accept any more incoming.

I remember wondering if it wouldn't have been better for me to be gone...to run away and never look back... to die and put an end to the madness I was no longer able to conceal. It was a serious thought.

Nothing was going my way, and nobody seemed to want to try and understand my pain. It wasn't their fault. I'd built my life around the lie I lived, again with such conviction that the truth was somewhat of a mystery to me, too. My corner of the ring was empty but for me, and I was a shell of the happy child of the Universe I once was. The reflections of days past only amplified my feelings of failure. I was the child of a mother who couldn't talk to me, a big sister who'd fallen from the pedestal she was once on, married to a man I didn't love and mother to four children I couldn't parent. My employer was losing patience with my circumstances and my need for days off (surgeries mostly but not all), and I was suddenly aware of how my condition touched on nearly every area of my life. I never seemed to respond to the challenges as quickly or as neatly as I might have. The Universe cuts no slack. It promises to give us all we need, and it is always on point, whether we are ready, or we are not.

I was not ready for the conversation my Mother had in mind.

Mom looked at me and asked if I was alright. I said 'Yes' but she didn't believe me, and I knew it. I was pale and thin and tired. Dark shadows adorned the areas under my empty eyes. I asked her if she was alright and she gave a half-smile. "I'm worried, Debby. I'm worried about your kids, and I am worried about you."

"I'll be okay, Mom." And for a moment, I felt my defenses rise. "I've managed to make it this far...and my kids are tough. They are tougher than I ever was."

There was silence for a moment. I waited for an argument, but there was none.

"Gregg came to see me yesterday" she said, softly and apologetically.

I wanted to roll my eyes, but I was too tired. My mother loved Gregg and if I'd have opened my mouth, something unforgiveable would have escaped.

I just stared at her, as if to say *'Okay, let me have it…there is nothing more you can say to change the direction of my slide into the hell I've created.'*

"He told me he thinks you are a lesbian."

She waited for my response and I was frantically searching for the right one, holding fast my blank stare as not to tip her off.

"Are you a lesbian, Debby?" her voice cracked, suggesting she was afraid to hear the answer.

"No" I said, and I felt traitorous to my beleaguered soul. I cleared my throat and put my head down to compose myself. I squirmed in my seat and wiped my tired eyes. I righted myself. I didn't know how to be truthful to both of us without damaging our relationship further; "I mean, I don't know …I really don't know, Mom" and at this point I was as close to being able to admit something to her…and to myself…as I had ever been, but I couldn't…because in my mind, the truth no longer mattered. *Did it ever?*

We were so close…for a brief pause, I could picture a breakthrough where we both might be saved. It was the perfect opportunity, but I couldn't follow through, and she couldn't help me. It quickly subsided. I was strangely comfortable with it resting along this well-traveled road. Our lives passed before me…the love, the sadness. In a very disturbing moment, I wondered if I could ever find happiness again…if all I'd ever known about life was all it ever could be…if God or Terry or any living loved one could save me, or even if I was worthy of saving.

"Do you want to talk about it?" she asked, and while I've no doubt this was a genuine gesture, I could see the uneasiness in her eyes...the same eyes that I associated with heartache.

I shook my head, no. My lips quivered. My shoulders dropped. She looked at me with such love and reassurance, but as much as I trusted her, I didn't trust us. Her eyes watered. I wanted to hold her. I believe she wanted to hold me. Instead, I squirmed in my chair and mouthed '*Sorry*.' After a short pause, I dug the cuff of my sleeve against my eyes to stop the tears before they could form. "I'll be okay...it will all be okay." I didn't believe it, and I'm certain she didn't either.

On my third trip to Harrisburg, Karen and I went to a birthday party for one of her friends. Truth be told, I had no desire to be there...or even in Harrisburg for that matter. I was 250 miles from my children, from my mother, from my job. I didn't know the 'birthday boy' nor had I met anyone else who would be there, apart from Karen who fervently insisted I attend. The larger part of me yearned to be alone, to lie in bed and cover my head with a pillow, to wish for death. A stronger truth, though, compelled me to push through the funk I was in and stand tall. Quite possibly, the underlying factor was Karen herself. Carefree and wild as the day I'd met her, she was the older, braver, brassier and bossier sister. Whatever the relationship, it was always hard for me to say 'no' to her, and she knew it. She scared me a little, too.

The drive from home to Harrisburg was long and mundane. I had a lot on my mind, of course, convinced my children believed I'd deserted them. Their father was no doubt fostering the notion. I hadn't seen them in almost a week. It had been 16 months since I left, and my will hadn't strengthened...it had turned to mush. The kids seemed to have adapted well enough to the daily routine of my absence. I wanted them to be okay, of course, but on a more selfish note, I wanted more for 'us' to be okay. There is sometimes a great distance between what I want to be true and the reality of what is, of course. On this particular weekend, though, they were at a family reunion with their father; quite excited for the pause in drama we'd imposed upon them. I knew they would not be spared the questions, assumptions, and criticisms pertaining to their absent mother. The comments would, no doubt, ricochet and reverberate for years to come, and I carried every scenario with me on the four-hour drive to Pennsylvania's capitol. By the time I arrived in Harrisburg, the children were all scarred, young adults with a series of crimes against humanity, and it was all my fault. Single handedly, selfishly, I'd managed to signal the end of the world.

The kids loved their father. They loved me, too, but at the time, someone had to be the villain, and I was the most likely. When they were with their Dad, they would spend the day playing and running and exploring as kids do, but then I would get home from work and everything turned into a war zone. Never mind the brutality of our relationship, our home was all they knew. It was me who couldn't continue. Something my mother said to me when I told her I would not return to Gregg played again and again in my head; "It's just that you never finish, Debby. You never see things through."

Once settled in at Karen's, I tried to wiggle out of my commitment to go to the party. We talked about old times, and about the dark secret she and only a handful of others knew...I was indeed a lesbian.

Though it might be easy to prove contrary, I do not believe my sexual orientation was born of circumstance. Abandoned by my birth father, molested by an older boy, and struggling for an equal place in my adopted father's heart, some might conclude otherwise, but looking back, I think in my gut I knew it all along. The only 'choice' I made was not to act on it. Often, I pushed away thoughts suggesting my adverse sexual preference

90

as though it was a stage I was going through. I read a couple articles suggesting most men and women questioned their sexuality at some point, and with my aptitude for taking longer to understand such things, I'd assumed I was just a typical female...delayed.

As time passed, this line of thinking was outwearing its usefulness. The Universe was screaming for my attention, suddenly introducing people and circumstances onto the path in front of me. Would I make peace with the person I was meant to be, or should I take the safer road to make peace with family and friends? Either way held a risk.

Frankly, my mind was leaning toward the latter when Karen abruptly jumped from the couch and declared, "Enough of all this shit, Livingston, we're going to a party!"

I was not prepared to act on my new lifestyle when I walked into the dimly lit studio apartment on Harris Street. Apparently, the Universe wanted me to push forward, but I was afraid and unsure of how to proceed. It sensed my deliberation and carried me. There were easily a dozen people gathered for Danny's birthday, including Karen and me. The energy of the room was spirited, and I was almost immediately intimidated by it. My state of mind was not on par with the seedy, smoldering atmosphere, either.

Suddenly, though, an abrupt infusion of light splayed across the room. It was coming from my right and pierced through the smoke-filled apartment not unlike a shaft of fairy dust. Like a glittered golden sunray, it swept directly through every object in its path and landed in the lap of someone sitting at a dining table to my left. No one else seemed to notice, but it captured my attention. Everything and everyone else in the room faded in sight and sound. The mysterious energy pulled me toward its focus, and I seemed unable or unwilling to challenge it. The lap belonged to a young woman named Sue, and with a simple glance, something magical stirred inside of me.   Fate enthusiastically and cryptically moved me toward her, and with lightning speed.

There was some conversation echoed toward me by others; "Hi! Nice to meet you, Debby, blah, blah, blah", but with so much gravitational pull to her space, I didn't own the where-to-for to respond with more than a nod to their niceties. A curious feeling of raw eagerness was forming deep within my being. It wasn't physical, but it manifested itself as such; goosebumps, and hair raising on my arms, a subtle reminder from somewhere within to steady myself, a meteor shower of sensitivities sanctioned by a greater authority....so powerful, I felt no inclination to resist...it overpowered me. I took a chair next to hers. Without much prodding, we exchanged brief bios of our collective past. She was from the Little League Capitol of the world, Williamsport, Pa. I was from a steel mill town, once a formidable competitor in the aluminum industry. We briefly discussed our families, our careers and our heterosexual experiences. She had been married for 7 years when she called it quits. It took me double that time to gather the courage to leave my husband. She had a daughter, Tiffany, a freshman in college. I had four children, the oldest, then 14, and the youngest, five.

Conversation flowed, fueled by vodka and tonic, and I felt a strange peace come over me. I was in the perfect place at the perfect time. It felt like a dream, but it wasn't. The night went on. I barely noticed Karen engaged in conversation with a woman name Jan. Just about the time I thought to ask Sue for her phone number, Karen announced it was time to leave. But, as we gathered ourselves to exit, Sue handed me her phone number scribbled on a book of matches. "Call me if you ever get back to Harrisburg" she said. "I really enjoyed talking with you." We hugged and I felt an even greater convergence of divine magnitude.

I was awestruck.

The following morning, Karen and I left for her childhood home in Lewistown. Karen was markedly uneasy for whatever had taken hold of her, as well, and I sensed an inner conflict for whatever she was feeling. She'd just always been a loner, comfortable with her status, clinging to the safety it provided. Her transparent cloak of humility under attack, barely able to contain all of who she professed to be, exposing what she felt to be a damnable flaw—just like everyone else, she needed to be loved.

The ride was unmistakably quiet, and I was happy not to talk. I couldn't shake the feeling I'd left my chance for future happiness in the rearview mirror. About halfway there, she broke the silence. "Everything okay?" she asked, in a tone that would suggest she knew everything not to be okay.

"Yeah, I'm fine" was my simple response.

"Mom will be happy to see you" she said, and for a moment I thought about arguing with her. The last time I went to visit I stayed for 90 days. It always felt like Betty was looking right through me, and I shuddered at the risks Karen and I took when we were younger. Unbeknownst to Betty (perhaps?), her eldest daughter and I had shared more than a bedroom. Betty was a by-the-book stoic German Catholic. There simply aren't enough *Hail Mary(s)* to account for what was going on in her house those few months.

Back then, it was Karen who seemed to know what she wanted out of life. I was just an aimless kid, four to five years her junior. She taught me much about life away from home and about sex, too. Again, the secrets we had between us would never be part of our conversation. Not. Ever. Anyway, Betty was waiting at the door for us when we pulled up in front of the house. She was smiling but I could see it wasn't without some effort. It was going to be a long day.

We had an enjoyable lunch, nonetheless. On the way home, Karen broke the stillness, "Mom asked if you were alright...and I told her that you were just missing your kids."

My heart felt a familiar jab when she mentioned the kids, but I'd painfully learned how to miss them for longer periods of time. My job carried me all over the northeastern corridor for extended stays, sometimes as lengthy as two weeks. Karen knew this. Still, I didn't argue the point. I was feeling sorry for myself. I realized how unreasonable I was acting, but I was unable to shake it. It was difficult to make the simplest of organized noises. I nodded in lieu of making the wrong one.

"You sure you don't want to talk about it?" she prodded, with a hint of reluctance.

I nodded yes.

For the next 30 or so minutes, the only sounds we heard were the humming of tires on grated roads, and the rhythmic thumps of the black strips between slabs on Highway 322. A car passed us, and this was remarkable enough since Karen was rather proud of her lead foot. When it pulled in front of us, though, the license plate read 9393. My fascination with numbers has always been a little extreme, and these series of digits caused me to smile. I was just about to offer up a comment because the day before was September 3. It was also my mother's birthday. Just as I began to think the Universe was demanding my attention, Karen interrupted.

"Okay, what the hell is wrong with you, Livingston?" It was a request born of frustration, not so much compassion.

To underline, Karen easily intimidated me. My focus shifted, almost mid-transformation, and I quickly tried to adjust.

"I'm serious, damnit, what's got you all bottled up? And, don't give me none o' your shitty *'nothings'*, either."

She emphasized 'nothings' with a rather condescending and slightly agitated tone. My veneer cracked. I was familiar with that attitude. Speech needed to manifest from my mouth, or I won't make it across the Clarks Ferry Bridge.

"I don't know, Karen. I...I think I just don't want to talk about it." There was second of hesitation to recall and sort through my thoughts. "I really don't know, I guess…" I plead with my most pathetic voice, "…maybe I just drank too much."

"No shit!" she offered in response. And then, "Is it that woman from last night?" she paused, but only briefly. "She got you all tied up in knots?"

For all the time that I had known Karen, this was a first for this topic. We'd never even had a conversation about our own love affair. Also, the hysteria of my circumstances usually brought out the calm in her. I didn't want her to think I was being ridiculous, certainly, but I also knew she would be honest with me. Our history together had provided me such assurance. Maybe I loved her so much because I trusted her so unequivocally. Suddenly, as though she'd just had an amusing thought, she slapped my knee and bore a toothy grin. Our bond was special, and, in that moment, I knew nothing had changed, and nothing ever would. She was genuinely concerned, and in a protective sort of way. She knew me. She read me like a book.

"Yes, I think so."

There was a long, and thoughtful pause before she responded. She stared straight ahead at the road in front of her.

"Then why don't you call her?" she said.

"Should I?" I mumbled, wishfully.

She cocked her head and squinted her eyes at me and said "Duh, let me think about it, Livingston." She sighed.

"Okay" I responded, feeling a little silly.

Once home, we unloaded some packages and climbed down the back stairs to her apartment on North Front St. She popped open a lite beer, handed it to me, and pointed to the phone. "Get on it, Livingston....in this world, someone like her isn't going to be on the market for very long."

"What do you mean? Do you know her?"

"I've seen her around. Mostly at the bar. I don't know her, personally, but I know some of the people she hangs around with.

They're good people...respectable; discriminating enough not to let just anybody into their little group. I don't know what the hell she sees in you, though" she finished with a laugh.

"She has a little group?" something just short of a giggle followed.

Karen grinned. It was the same look I succumbed to all those years ago. The one that never failed me. When she smiled, and especially when she smiled at me, I felt so thoroughly loved and, more importantly, safe. She could take the black and white of any situation and find all the colors and magic of looking through a kaleidoscope. She saw the world like I wanted *in the worst way* to see it.

I picked up the phone before I even realized what I was going to say. *I hate when this happens.*

"Hello!" There was no mistaking the voice on the other end of the line.

96

"Hi, is this Sue?" My nerves caught up to my actions. *What if she didn't feel the same way? What if she didn't even remember me?*

"Yes," she responded neatly.

"Hey…Sue, this is Debby. We met last night at the birthday party?"

There was a brief pause. "Hi" was her short, and puzzled response.

"Hi, um, I was wondering if you were…um, if you umm….if you were going to be at the bar tonight…"

I was feeling optimistic.

"No" she replied firmly, almost defiantly, and my heart sunk, along with what remained of my nerves.

I've never been the pursuer. I'm too clumsy. Never in my life have I asked someone on a date. Still, I was sure less than 16 hours ago my life had been transformed and lifted to heights I'd never realized! I thought she felt it too. I was so confident this was my next move! *Had I held in my heart the card of disillusionment? Did the booze get to me more than I thought?*

"Oh! Umm, okay…" I didn't know where to go from here, and the next two syllables could easily have been mistaken for three; "o-o—kay."

"Wait!" she interrupted, "What?! (pause) Do you mean with you?" And if I was totally surprised by the first exchange, this left me completely caught off guard, but quick to respond.

"Yes" I answered a little too eagerly.

She laughed. "I'm sorry, I thought you'd already gone back to W.Va. I get tired of the bar scene, but I would love to meet you there. 8:00?"

97

Within three months, I took residence in Pennsylvania.

CHAPTER 10

Sue and I...

...entered into Holy Union on a beautiful early June afternoon. We'd been living together for over a year and a half, unphased mostly, with the on again - off again rulings for gay marriage, for equality in every area for the LGBTQ communities. Our nuptials were provided by and presided over by the Reverend Eva O'Diem of Harrisburg's MCC Ministries. We went through many of the same motions and rituals of a traditional wedding, but other than the commitment we made between God, ourselves and our friends, the ceremony had little legal merit. At the time, it hardly mattered. We came to accept our place in the world because we could see it moving forward, however slow the gain. We were excited to share our vows with those of like mind and spirit at the Quaker House in downtown Harrisburg.

The LGBTQ community has experienced the same difficulties facing other minorities in our country. From meeting in dark nightclubs under the guise of 'private' establishments to congregating in hideaway fields and/or parks under the ruse of camping, or sharing quarters as 'roommates', many found ways to refrain from the real-life threats for acting on who we were. Each had a different reality for why and when we chose to come clean. Mine was simple. I was tired of pretending. I wasn't on a mission to save anyone else, or to make excuses for those who'd betrayed the conventional union between a man and a woman. My heart was sick with dread for the way I felt. I spent a lot of time and misery avoiding my true nature, but I couldn't stop feeling it.

My life hurdled another impasse, and it was impossible to do it alone. I felt like a steel marble in a pinball machine. The most important people in my life were pulling me in one direction and the Universe in another. The truth for who I was couldn't fit into the box my family and friends reserved for me. The truth kept landing me in the same narrow slot from where I began. Pull and shoot, pull and shoot. I didn't just wake up 'gay' one day. I did wake up one day to embrace it.

I was at a Gay Pride event once when a heckler made a comment about God's wrath for our abomination unto Him. "Have you thought about what you are going to say to the Almighty God when He asks you to explain your heathen ways?" he bellowed with fire and brimstone in his voice. I lifted my head, but I did not respond. I haven't lowered my head since. But, have I thought about it? Yes...and here is what I will say should the Almighty God in all his anger ask me such a question. "Dear God...if this offends you so, why did you make me this way?"

The real point is, though, I've taken all my cues from the Universe...from God. It took me longer than it should have because I initially, errantly believed the people preaching to me cared more or knew more for my life than my Creator did. I spent a lifetime following a road paved for others...ignoring the path God made for me.

It has been said we shall atone for our sins when the grim reaper comes for us. Believe what you want, but there is no grim reaper coming for me; I will be escorted off this planet in the same manner for which I am accustomed to traveling here...on the wings of angels. However, should I be asked to atone for my crimes, I am ready. I've been practicing for most of my life.

The only friend I'd invited (Lisa) was unable to attend, but I had no shortage of new friends to show support for my newest and bravest adventure. Sue invited many friends to the nuptials, and it was a packed house. Neither of us invited our families, not even the children, because of the uncertainty of how it would affect them, or more importantly, how it would influence our future with them.

Our children and our families were all aware of our sexual preference and were supportive to the extent we weren't shunned at family gatherings, but human nature had proven time and again, full and successful integration and mutual respect could only be answered satisfactorily through trial and time. The coming months and years provided both but make no mistake; we worked harder for the achievements than the heterosexuals introduced to our families. Beyond our vows, we privately made only one commitment; we would never raise a hand to the other. Sue and I had both suffered with violence in our past relationships. We lived up to our promise easy enough.

We would be tested in a myriad of other ways, however.

Within a few months of our vows, Gregg suffered a double brain aneurism. He survived, but he would need months of skilled care. Sue and I brought the 3 youngest children to live with us (Shelley refused to leave her father and was old enough to stay with family friends...she was also still upset with me). I was thrilled at the prospect of having my kids with me under one roof. Sue was not. Still, day after day, she would rise early to get them off to school when I couldn't be there to tend to their needs. My work often demanded me to be away for days at a time, and even when I was home, I needed to leave earlier for work than they were scheduled for school.

Jessica was in middle school and Kelsey (six) was in the first grade; Chip, 'just shy' of five years old was in pre-school. The two youngest did adjust, but Jessica struggled. She tried so hard to wear a brave face, but she resented being taken from her father, wasn't exactly fond of her new stepmother, and was very defensive when Sue raised her voice to her younger siblings. I phoned home at least twice daily, and the tension between Sue and Jessica was paramount. I tried to reassure them both, even when I had little hope myself. Tempers flared on more than one occasion.

I entered the back door of our Middletown duplex to find Sue straddling atop Jessica, pinning her to the floor and screaming at her. I screamed at Sue and ran for my little girl. Jessica wasn't crying. Her face was purple with anger. "Sue," I yelled in a panic, feeling my own temper rise as I pulled her off of the child "what are you doing?" They glared at each other, both in defensive mode...both begging me for a favorable response. How could this have gone so terribly wrong?

It turns out my sweet child went after Sue (she was nearly as tall, and probably outweighed her stepmother). Sue took her down to avoid her going 'bat shit crazy' and hurting herself. Knowing I was soon to be home, she kept her there until I arrived or until Jessica composed herself. I arrived well ahead of that...just about a day ahead.

Add to Sue's situation the stress of a full-time job, help with homework needed by the kids, and the daily room-to-room chase with Chip (he thought it was a game, and had it not been for the fury over her situation, I think Sue might have thought the same), and a daily dose of excitement provided by my ever-adventurous-and-curious youngest daughter, Kelsey.

It was second nature for me to check the hotel's front desk for messages upon my return from daily training meetings. I was in a small town outside of Atlanta, Georgia, for a team building exercise when a dutiful but nervous desk clerk met me at the door. "You have an emergency phone call" she said. "A lady named Sue has called twice! I saw your shuttle pull up" she added, apologetically.

"Oh my God" was all I could muster as I ran past her, handing off my brief case in route. Another clerk was standing at the desk holding the phone out to me. "Hello" I said, out of breath and rising with dread. My hands were perspiring.

It was Sue. "I swear to God…." She started and I actually breathed a sigh of relief because of her tone. She certainly wouldn't be calling to tell me there'd been an accident or a murder starting with "I swear to God".

"What? What is it? What's wrong?" I said, simultaneously changing my mood from dread to anger.

"It's Kelsey again!" she proclaimed. "Everything is okay now, but I had the phone in my hand to call the fire department! I can't take any more of this!" and now she was in tears.

"What happened?" I sighed, switching back to dread.

"How many times have we told them not to go out onto the balcony because it isn't safe?" she pleaded. "I sealed the window to deter them, and she walked right through the freaking door."

"I know, but, how…" I began to ask. The door had been inoperable for years; jammed shut. Sue nor I had been able to open it.

"She just opened the door and walked right through it, Debby…She went through the damned door and it shut behind her and it jammed again, and we couldn't get it open…Jessica came running down the stairs screaming, and …Oh My God!!"

"Oh geesh," I replied in complete resignation.

It didn't get any better the next couple of months. On another occasion, Kelsey (again with this kid) was sleep-walking in the middle of the night, picked up the phone, dialed random numbers and awakened a panicked and unforgiving couple. They retrieved the number and called Sue. It was 3:00 in the morning and they were less than apologetic for returning the favor.

Our largest hurdle, though, was one we couldn't clear. They missed their Dad, terribly, and worried over not being with him. His mother was doing her part to keep the kids upset, but I do not believe this was her intent. She missed the children also, and just wanted them to come home. She and I had clashed on many an occasion and I refused to talk to her (childish behavior on my part, I agree). According to the kids, their grandmother would come and get them, and *don't tell your mother*! (How little she must know my kids to think they could keep a secret!) She went on to say how much their Dad missed them – "he won't be able to get better till you return..."

My ex-mother-in-law lived several hours away, and while I truly believed she thought she was just proving her love to the kids and had no real intention for picking them up at school, she'd had a history of doing some pretty desperate things (modestly speaking).

'So Hum'...'Ohm'...'

Deep breath...here goes.

A few months after I left Gregg, I was nominated to receive recognition from the State of W.Va. Board of Rehabilitation Services (disability). I was treated to a night's stay and a ceremony with dinner in the state's capitol in Charleston, along with a meeting with Governor Caperton's wife, Rachael Worby. The basis of the award was to distinguish my efforts for work above and beyond the limitations of my lifelong anomaly. It was a big deal. I took my oldest girls, Shelley and Jessica, along with another manager who'd helped me along the way. My District Manager, D, also attended, per invitation.

All went well. I am a decent speaker but didn't spend too much of everyone's time. We did the celebratory dinner and returned home.

A few weeks later, on a Sunday afternoon, I received a call from my boss. His voice was shaking. A faxed letter from a business center at a terminal in the Pittsburgh Airport was received by our corporate headquarters, claiming my boss and I were having an affair, among other insidious accusations that shall remain a secret to protect the innocently accused. The letter demanded we both be fired, or pictures taken at the hotel where the conference in Charleston was held would be published to support the claim and embarrass the company. This I knew to be nonsense, of course, but my company didn't know any more about my personal life, apparently, than they did about the sender.

A security team from headquarters was dispatched to Pittsburgh and would be interviewing the two of us. They would also request any and all photographs and receipts from the business office inside the airport where the facsimile was originated. They had an idea of who the sender was, but verification, of course, was necessary. My company requested and received a grainy photo taken at the sending station. The photo resembled an older woman in a coat with a scarf on her head, wearing sunglasses.

My boss, who I'll refrain from naming, was a good and highly respected young man. He was as upset as I was over this horrible accusation. From the vague description we'd been given, we believed the sender to be someone within the company who was passed over for advancement in lieu of my promotion. I was shocked, as the woman was a friend.

An impressive and sophisticated group of investigators, along with corporate attorneys and representatives were ordered to board a jet immediately to get to the bottom of the matter. From the standpoint of what it must have cost, alone, I understood the seriousness of the matter.

We were told to tell no-one; to continue business as usual until all the information was gathered. We were also warned to avoid contact with each other...'threatened' might be a better definition. I did tell someone, though...I told Gregg.

Per my new orders, I was sent to set a store in Niagara Falls, NY. On the job by myself, I was more than a little nervous, not so much for the outcome which I knew to be completely false, but about the rumors that might persist for me being an unfit parent, or even as a human being should the name of the accuser not be identified, the mere speculation attached to my reputation.

On my third day of setting the store, a security guard summoned me to the entrance. I had a visitor. It was Gregg. We were easily 3-4 hours from our hometown. "I need to talk to you, Deb" he said, and my face must have looked as frightened as I was. He quickly added "the kids are okay, Debby, the kids are fine...but I need to talk to you about something." Before it was through, he told me that it had been his mother who'd written the letter and faxed it. I was furious...livid! "Are you kidding me?" It took me a moment to speak without anger. "Your mother did this?" I was in utter disbelief! "Are you freaking kidding me, Gregg?!"

Gregg pleaded with me not to press charges. "Please, Debby, I'm begging you" he said over and over.

"She just wanted you to come back home. I know it's twisted...you know how she is...but for the kids' sake, Deb, please don't press charges."

Gregg was devastated and scared. He trembled. He cried. Eventually, I buckled, but I told him I didn't know how the company would react. There had been a small fortune put into this already. I called my boss immediately after Gregg left and his response held both relief and concern: "...and I may get fired, Debby. It's not your fault and it's not my fault, but if you don't press charges, I cannot guarantee they wouldn't see you as a liability."

I didn't know what to do. Why? Why? Why was this happening to me? I'd worked so hard, given up so much, and this was my reward? Why was the Universe punishing me?

After a few moments, his tone softened further. He was sympathetic to my situation, and added; "Debby, listen...it's your call. If you do not wish to press charges, I won't press charges either. I just can't promise you things won't backfire on the two of us...but I understand...I truly understand. I don't know what will happen. I really don't, but this has got to be hard for you. Do what you must, but you've only got a couple of days to decide." Sometimes the nicest people in the world to me are the people who have the least to benefit. The Universe was alive and well...another angel identified.

I do not know for certain whether he was fired or transferred, but he was gone the following week. To avoid the possibility of being vanished on bad terms, I gave my notice and that's when I called my friend Karen.

As for my ex-mother-in-law's behavior; with her husband gone and her only child in the hospital, Sue and I believed she was emotionally fragile and capable of just about anything. We made certain one of us was there to pick up the children when school was let out.

Within four months, Gregg was discharged from a rehab facility. He wasn't completely well, but he was alive and able to maneuver about with a little help. I gave our children the option (did I really have a choice?), and they chose to be with their Dad. It was a difficult situation for me, but it was a lot harder for them. I couldn't allow my selfishness to overrule their collective hearts. As much as it pained me, I supported their decision and took them home. But I was angry and sullen with Sue, convinced she'd made it difficult for them to want to stay. It didn't matter, and I knew it, but I was aching. They missed their Dad and they needed to know he was okay. He needed them even more, and we all knew that, too.

Within a year, my oldest came to live with us. Shelley was sixteen and mad as hell. As pretty as a rose, this child of mine brought with her one bag of clothes and a case full of thorny discontent.

I couldn't be mad at her; she just needed proof I loved her. She'd gotten the shitty end of a bad deal, but as it was, I had no magic to fix the mess I made. I prayed. I cried. I tried to reason with her. I fought with Sue. Sue fought with Shelley. I paid for counseling sessions; Shelley refused to talk. I met with school officials: Shelley refused to talk. The problems between Sue and Shelley mounted to the extent I had to find other accommodations for my daughter and myself. We rented a nice little garage apartment about a mile away and within two months we were promptly evicted when one of the owners smelled marijuana in the stairwell. Of course, I was at work, and Shelley insisted it wasn't her. Of course, I believed her. Of course, I shouldn't have.
Anyway, back to living with Sue, and Shelley seemed to calm down for a little while. The arguments between the two continued but I was almost numb to the effect. It didn't seem to matter what I said anyway. I was a terrible referee.

Within a year, though, all hell broke loose.

It had been a hard winter. There was just about six feet of snow piled up outside our doorway, but on the 26th of January the outdoor temperature soared to nearly 80 degrees. The snow melted and then it rained. We lived about 40 feet from a small creek near the town of Selinsgrove, a charming little place in Pennsylvania's mid-section. The flood happened so fast, the kids at the high school who lived on the other side of the creek

108

couldn't get home and Shelley had been with a couple of them. Sue and I were evacuated from our home and invited to stay with my boss and his wife until it was safe to go back. The Comfort Inn was nice enough to let the kids stay there until arrangements could be made to get to them.If only the group of kids my daughter was with could have been more grateful. The police were called. The kids broke into the bar at the hotel and stole liquor. Since Shelley was the youngest of the group, and since she was the only one without a police record, she was 'volunteered' to be the ruse. Of course, she accepted, and after an 'All Points Bulletin' (APB) was issued, she was arrested along with one other student.

She plead 'no contest'. Due to the status of her age, she was put on probation.

Her record was expunged on her 18th birthday.

Mercifully, my boss, (Gene) transferred me back to Harrisburg. He also hired Sue as Assistant Manager at my location pending my next transfer. Shelley switched schools and after a few months dropped out of school altogether.

This isn't a story about a kid gone bad. Shelley's story doesn't end here. Her time to shine for the amazing person she has always been would be celebrated at a later date. It appears the Universe seeks to brighten the light in all of us.

It wouldn't be the last time the police would be involved. Through the trials and the troubles, little joy was to be found, but there was always a candle burning with hope in my heart. Shelley and Sue couldn't get out of each other's way and I was working double time trying to give of my time to each of them. Time would prove I couldn't. I worked, often away from home for days at a time, and I never tried to get out of it. Emotionally, I needed these respites to maintain any sense of sanity.

Physically, I was battling one surgery after another; my body was showing its wear and tear, and spiritually, I was running on empty. Financially, there was no way to support any of them if I couldn't continue to work.

In the meantime, the three younger kids visited us often enough for Sue to be accepted into their new family situation. It took time and it took patience; the latter of which Sue seemed slower to yield than the children. It was hard for her, but despite my dodging the issues, she worked her magic through them, or the kids were relentless with the love they showed her. There were times I'd watch them laugh with one another and be overcome with joy, but never enough to trust it would last. I was always waiting for the other shoe to drop. We never ran out of shoes.

Sue and I argued often. We disagreed on the way we parented, specifically with discipline (and lack thereof). Neither of us struck the kids, but the punishment for minor offenses could last the entire visit, and with four underage children, there were endless opportunities for wrongdoings to occur. I was willing to overlook most as 'kids will be kids.' Sue was not. Her history with her own child proved to be much different.

Tiffany is Sue's only child. If all parents could be so lucky! Kind, compassionate, considerate, smart, personable and GOOD, this child might have been dubbed for sainthood had she not had one genetic flaw...one I was slow to understand. The syndrome caused her to be inordinately tidy with her belongings, unable to leave clothes unfolded or on the floor, no toothpaste in the sink or dirty dishes either, no ring around the inside of the tub. She was an excellent student, respectful of others, delightful to be around and respectful. When she wasn't getting an education, she was working and earning her own way. I loved Tiffany within days of being introduced to her. It would be a challenge for anyone capable of loving to feel otherwise.

Life was moving fast in the years to follow. I struggled to keep up. My mother called to say she was remarrying, Sue was suffering, woefully, with a condition the doctors would eventually call clustered migraines, I was transferred to a location sixty miles north of Harrisburg. With little time to prepare, I was instructed to attend a team building event for work in Georgia as I'd been selected, once again, to be recognized for my work. Every high came with a low...each time I was given a great opportunity to expand my professional horizons, another part of my life would unravel. When things were going well at home, problems would manifest in the workplace. In hindsight, I can see where the Universe was going with all of this, but at the time I felt defeated, and I had little incentive to give thanks.

Within a couple of months, my mother was diagnosed with non-Hodgkin's lymphoma.

When she first told me about the diagnosis, I cried. This, in and of itself, was remarkable. As tragic the news, my ability to let my emotions show to her had been forty years in the making. But, just as the tears came, she told me the doctor felt optimistic about her chances; the prognosis was good. She would need chemotherapy, but she would be okay. So adept is my inclination to turn things around...to manipulate the underlying truth into a positive outcome. I went from tears to celebration mode within 30 seconds. I made a couple trips home to see her and she seemed to be coping well. The chemo had visibly taken a toll on her, but according to her, the doctors said it was working.

I went to visit her over the Memorial Day weekend and before I arrived, she was admitted with an infection. When I walked through the back door to an empty house, something felt not right. My sister called to tell me Mom was in Steubenville's Trinity Hospital. I went to see her, and she was feeling miserable. She told me she wanted to stop the chemo...she was too tired...she couldn't do it anymore. I tried to improve upon her outlook, and thought I'd succeeded, but she would be gone within two weeks. For all the experiences, good and bad, this event would deliver the deepest impact on my life. It never occurred to me this would be the last I'd see her.

In the grand scheme of things, my faith has quietly allowed me to escape most regrets and surrender the guilt attached to them. I have come to understand, truly, that the messes I've made and even the messes made for me were necessary evils in my development, along with a personal resolve to do better. I've forgiven myself for all of them. This one, though...

My mother was 64 years old when she left this world.

CHAPTER 11

Reflection is imminent, of course...

...if you wish to test yourself for authenticity. After my mother died, a great unsettling began in me. Looking back, I believe this was my first real understanding of a higher consciousness; my 'God' mind. I'd experienced spiritual awareness and mindfulness over the years from time to time, but God seemed to be giving me extra attention at about this juncture, perhaps because I was open to it, or maybe because I felt desperate enough to latch onto anything. Sue believed I was in the middle of an emotional breakdown, and though it took time and convincing, she came to understand my highs and lows to be a necessary step in my spiritual cleansing. Never had my conviction been met with such profound evidence, not that God existed—I'd always believed that—but that He was pulling the strings; in nature and timing, love and forgiveness, patience and understanding, situations and circumstances; in me. I do not pretend to be God. I do profess to be a part of Him, though, and He a part of me. I couldn't use my mother as my crutch. I was an extension of her physically, yes, but I was also eternally tied to the love we shared. That love was conflicted, but it was also stronger than life. It transcended my ability her absence. This was truly an epiphany for me.

The indications may sound practical, and even inevitable for someone who relied so heavily on the love of a parent, but I'd not had the courage to visit such thoughts before she was gone. Enter the Universe. It suddenly and most naturally occurred to me to be a waste of time to support any other scenario. The spirit of my mother visited me on occasion. Momma made an appearance now and then, and Terry, of course, too. My Dad showed up in a couple of dreams to tell me he wasn't really dead, though, and this is when the notion hit me with the power of the proverbial runaway train.

Was everybody gone not really dead?

Suddenly aware of each step, and of the magical power provided of my God consciousness, I began to actively search for answers to my marvelous and miraculous, precocious and somewhat painful life. A plethora of questions initiated from that consciousness; from the Universe. First, who was I without my mother? Without Momma and Dad and Terry? It would take some time to figure it out. I was nothing without them. Sometimes, I felt overwhelmed with their spiritual intrusions and other times I tried to push them away. But it continued, despite the arguments I offered against it. The Universe was persistent, patient...and creative. They left me the best part of themselves, and the opportunity to build the best of me with what remained of them.

Once upon a time, and before thinking 'outside the box' became an everyday intention for me, I was approached by a young lady at a birthday party. She had flowers in her hair. She was a hippie, I guess, an observation based solely on her attire and how I perceived her to move about the room. She glided...or floated? Her body moved but there was no visible indication she had feet. Her large bell-bottomed jeans barely skimmed the surface of the floor and her feet never extended beyond the edge of the hem. Her name was Priscilla and she may or may not have been noteworthy to anyone else. She was graceful, and her warm eyes were a translucent green. I found myself gawking at her for reasons I couldn't explain. She caught me, mid-stare, probably with my mouth open, and she drifted towards me. I braced myself for a confrontation regarding my rude ogling and/or dazed expression, mortified and stuttering with my thoughts even before my mouth could form a dignified

114

response. Her voice was as soft and soothing as a lullaby. "Did anyone ever tell you that you are surrounded by angels?" she questioned. Did I hear a harp playing in the background?

Seriously, it was as though she sang the words to me.

"Ummm...uh... well, yeah" I said, awkwardly. "...I hear that a lot."

She smiled and nodded as though she was certain of my response, folded her hands and said with a liquid voice and a bow of her head, "Namaste", an ancient Hindu term meaning "The God in me recognizes the God in you". I did not know it then. I thought it was Hippie talk for 'peace and love'. My assumption was pretty much on point.

Priscilla turned to walk away; then paused and turned toward me once again. Her eyes were glistening as though she'd just remembered something, and I was reminded again of her fascinating persona. She looked at me with a measure of excitement and said in that same operatic voice, "Your mother says to tell you she loves you."

What?

Her unsolicited observation regarding the angels who highlighted the energy around my body initially struck me with a familiar feeling. I had it. I thought about it on occasion. I never spoke of it. But, when she mentioned my mother, I could barely contain myself. The result of this otherwise innocent mesmerizing encounter left me feel a little lighter...freer...bolder...and connected to something greater! It must be a sign! I tried to glide, though, and tripped over a lawn chair (also a sign).

Otherworldly interruptions of this nature weren't something new for me, but to this juncture I'd managed to greet them with questions, then dismiss them with logic. Throughout my life, people have inexplicably been drawn to me. There were approximately 50 people at this gathering, but this kind and gentle stranger weaved her way through a crowded room with clusters of guests and scattered pieces of furniture to talk to me. Me! It was as if she was looking, specifically, for me. Why? How did she find me? Did she have some kind of personal esoteric sensory device for navigation? Like a map?

A map? Is there a map? Do I have a map? If so, how can I make use of it? Was it too late? Was I too lost? How far off the trail might I have wandered? In a flurry, pictures of my life flashed in my mind. It occurred to me I couldn't have skipped any of the circumstances in my life without some navigational wherewithal, and land at this place in this time. Every map is different, I guessed. I'd simply taken the road less traveled.

In this sense 'everything' that happened to this end mattered. Every person I met, every circumstance I encountered, every moment I lived...it all mattered. My mother couldn't have been more unlike me on the surface, yet I respected and appreciated and loved her as though she was my mentor. And what about everyone else? They were all relevant to my purpose. Accidents, mistakes, out of the blue occurrences---each a part of the reason I was here. I'd been approached by strangers on numerous occasions with remarkable commentary regarding my 'aura'. What's more, people seemed to genuinely like me...almost immediately. The mosaic of my life was pulling together...all the little bits and pieces of previously unsought revelations were suddenly tickling my curious nature.

Why? Why do birds appear to be speaking to me? Why do I hear the trees whisper my name? What kind of banana peel allows me to slip, then fall short of landing in my grave (repeatedly)? Am I lucky or blessed or both? For the first time in my life, I gave notice to all the things I'd taken for granted...cackling birds and chattering squirrels, the unfolding of blossoming roses, the smell of spring and the slap of winter's cold breeze on my cheeks; timing of events and the numbers on my digital clock somewhat consistently displaying 11:11, 1:11, 2:22 and so forth. Moments with extension.

I saw my surroundings from a different perch: from that of an untethered child. I needed answers, and I realized some very relevant truths. There were no accidents. There were no coincidences, and nothing was trivial. Everything on my plate needed eaten, or at least, tasted. The Universe played along and subtly provided me clues and urges and situations and circumstances. It was as though I was participating in a scavenger hunt; the map and the points of interest delightfully (some, not delightfully) highlighted. With each discovery, a new clue and a new disclosure.

I explored my curiosities; I read books on angels (*I'm not one*), and animal totems (*mine is a crow*). I dabbled in sacred texts of various religions (dabbled might be an overstatement). I practiced guided meditation in search of spirit guides. And, then, I stumbled upon a website for Numerology.

If you took geometry in school, you may find the name Pythagoras to be familiar. (I never made it to geometry...I stayed stuck on first year algebra for three years.) He was a Greek philosopher and mathematician in the 6th century, noted for his deep faith, and genius mind, he was also a highly respected astrologer, tenacious researcher and Olympian. He taught high-caliber students in a school sometimes dubbed "secret society', strictly adhering to a teaching policy NOT to record anything (hence, secret in the society, explained). Between the lines of what I've read about him, he displayed some of the same characteristics of a prophet.

Pythagoras believed the Universe expressed itself through numbers (as did Einstein). His point was well measured with other theorists and historical colonies, i.e., the Hebrews, Babylonians and the Kabbalah. He is known today as the father of Numerology.

If Numerology isn't something you've given much credence, I'd highly recommend looking into it, for no other reason than you might find it entertaining. Do not be surprised, though, to discover incredible familiarity! I stumbled onto Numerology just a few years ago, in another half-hearted attempt to find relevant comparison for my strange, but true life. As someone so accustomed to living in the minority (spiritual manifestations, health, sexuality, adaptability, etc.), I've sometimes complained, and other times reveled in my weirdness. Numerology provided me some justification for said weirdness, and validation, too, for my soul's significance in the Universe.

Your Numerology life path number is based on the day you were born. Just add, then reduce to a single digit. (use your internet's search engine to find the meaning associated with your life path number). In the most fundamental of these numerological truths, you will find similarities. Keep reading and researching; get all the numbers and see what happens. It's like God's way of giving everyone equal bidding for adventure, and confirmation that you are where you are supposed to be on the path mapped out for you.

Life Path Equation example.

Date of Birth: July 16, 1999 =

7/16/1999 =

ADD: (7 + 1 + 6) plus (1+ 9 + 9 + 9) =

ADD: 14 + 28 = 42

REDUCE: 42 = 4 + 2 = Life Path 6

It's just an example. I am not a six (6). I am a nine (9).

It appears Mother Teresa, Mahatma Gandhi, and I have a little something in common: We are all a Life Path Nine (9); old souls, apparently. According to some numerological and metaphysical wizards, this is my last trip here...my last flowchart available without special dispensation, maybe? We each get nine lives, I'm told. If this is true, time is losing its sharp edge for me here (some might conclude, my mind is duller, too).

Nevertheless, I wish I'd have stumbled on to this numerology thing a little sooner, but Divine Timing being what it is and all...

There are moments I think I'd like to get the Universe's allowance for another chance, but mostly, I do look forward to leaving with the same excitement and sense of adventure that accompanied me here.

Yes, there are other Galaxies to adventure, I think.

The Universe communicates with me in a multitude of ways, and numbers are just one of them. Metaphors are another. The bible is full of them. I've deciphered some of the language, but I have been equally frustrated; enough to shake my fist at the Universe and scream, "What do you want from me?" This usually greets me with silence, or dismissal...*come back when you're ready to be rational, Debby*...other times, the proverbial slap to the side of my head. In times of reflection, I speak softer and deeper, and this is when the Universe responds in kind.

Through the course of my musings and meanderings, I've been accosted with questions I don't know how to answer. "Why does God let bad things happen to good people?" and "Why can't we all just be happy?" I venture to guess it's because we wouldn't appreciate what we have without something to measure it against. It begs the question; if I live in a perpetual state of happiness do I even know what it is? If I am a child of God who has agreed to experience the human existence, don't I want all I can get out of it? "If I live in a total state of bliss, am I living? Am I truly 'all in'?"

I don't put a lot of energy into saving the world, but I recycle, and I try to be kind, and I try not to give the world more reason to need saving. I don't give money much focus, either, but I like when I have it and so do my bill collectors. My thoughts have proven responsible for the part of destiny I control, and I've learned this truth the hard way.

I marvel how the Universe gets me on track when my direction is off. When I look through the doors of memory, the evidence of its power and timing are too incredible for me to resource a credible alternative. As for my thoughts, I choose to be happy...mostly...and mostly, I am. If I continue to think I'm happy, I don't need to change a thing...but when I hit a snag; I get aches and pains (part of the experience, I'm afraid), my rent is due, the car won't start and the doctor says 'I need to take some biopsies', I start to misplace the 'happy'...*it was here just a moment ago*.

I'm not a newbie. I've been around awhile; some might describe it an eternity. I watch, I listen, I learn. I find happiness comes from within, is escorted by appreciation, and grounded in good will. If my life is off-kilter, I need to foster some love and forgiveness for myself, some gratitude to the Universe, and some kindness for my neighbor. I've been slow to learn and at times slower to deliver, but I've never been disappointed with the outcome of this strategy once I've applied it.

Sometimes the Universal elements get churned up in the human ones, I guess; cause and effect, action and reaction. I don't know all the answers (yet), but I don't have to be a rocket scientist to know each element has contributed to my existence. I have a lot of questions. The Universe, no doubt, will, accordingly, provide me more of them. Every minute of every day throughout my journey, I have chosen to appreciate the experience I'm living, and I hope less for what I'm due and more for the treasures I think about.

I am so grateful for God and all the angels in my life.

Most likely, if you and I have crossed paths, you are one of them. My impeccably choreographed and perfectly flawed life couldn't have happened without a single one of you! If you have been positioned to be an impressionable part of my life, I acknowledge your 'Aye-Yai-Yai'...and thank you for your patience.

If you haven't had the occasion to reflect on these same truths, don't be too worried. Your life will happen in its own time, and when it does, it will be Divine. And let me offer you this, too: it is human nature to doubt the messages we get from the Universe. I still struggle with it, and argue with it, as though I know what's best. Whatever God has in store for me, though, is where I will ultimately land. This is an undeniable fact.

I think people tend to believe things they say and that they are a verbal extension of their thoughts. *I tend to think some of the things I say are nonsense, and too often I am right.* This line of thinking has served me well, though. I've heard people say 'life sucks' and I cringe (right after I duck and quietly work to remove myself from giving merit to their words). The Universe will acquiesce because you asked for it and it doesn't want to slap you around (too much). Still, people should be careful what they ask for. I've heard more than one person say, "my family comes first...before anything!" and then I watch as the Universe not only continues to provide situations to support those feelings, it will throw in circumstances to help them *'prove it!'* If we in the collective earnestly believe we want to save the world, the Universe will continue to give us a world that needs saving. The language isn't really that hard to understand, but the directives are a little catter-wocky sometimes, because in the end the Universe calls the shots.

It's a fine line for me...to make the most out of my life, and then save a little for those who come after me and want for the same. I don't give a lot of thought to wanting more, but when it comes, I'm happy, and when it doesn't, I give it equal play time for my mind to mull it over. I take into consideration, too, that I can't miss what I never had.

I've given careful consideration to the philosophy I was sent here for a purpose. Perhaps I am here to fulfill an obligation to others. Perhaps my experience here is to let go of old ideas and embrace new ones. Or, maybe I'm here to prove I can finish. Perhaps it is none or all of these things. But, if I really am here for the last time, I'm doing my best to appreciate every moment...even if every moment isn't meant for enjoyment.

I live near the sweetest place on earth; Hershey, Pa! Chocolate World, Hershey Museum, Hershey Amusement Park, did I mention chocolate? Okay, so if I take my grandchildren to the park for the day, I might expect to run into an occasional problem: Caiden will want to go the arcade with Elijah who doesn't want him tagging along. Then he'll want to go on the roller coaster with Peyton who will have a fit because she already has to take care of Jaycee; everybody wants something to eat but never at the same time and heaven forbid from the same food stand. Someone always needs escorted to the bathroom and before the day is through, at least one of the kids will vomit on my $100 sun shirt, another will need a bandage, and a security guard will be summoned when one of the children has wandered outside of the pre-set parameters. The day will drag on until we shut down all the rides, my feet burn and my back aches, and then we get to the car to find my keys locked inside.

Meanwhile, back on the home front, my adult children are sipping wine coolers, no doubt amused by my temporary insanity for taking the children in the first place. I will spend a ridiculous amount of money, and long after I've spent my last dime, the kids will be complaining about something they didn't get to do, or...everything else. Sounds fun, right? Yet, I do it, and we all get home safely, and everyone can't temper their excitement; *"it was so awesome!" "Momma got soaked!" (hahaha) "We had a blast!"* and the dreaded *"Can we go again next year?"*

And I say, *"Of course! [deep breath] Is there any more wine?"*

Sometimes it may be hard to swallow a pill suggesting we are all just spoiled and unsatisfied children of the Universe who volunteered to go to earth and play 'human'? We bitch and we complain and then the ride stops...and we want to go again.

CHAPTER 12

After a few more years...

...of climbing the corporate ladder, I worked my thoughts into a frenzy. I loved the work, mind you, but the 'woman vs. man' debate had me square in the middle of the argument, and more than a little frustrated. I'm all for living the dream, and I tried focusing on it, but there was always someone to train, and while I was happy to do it, within a few years, my location became the launch for 'men' destined to be ahead of me in line. It appeared that the only thing holding me back was my gender, *and my mother's concern; "it's just that you never finish, Debby."*

Bitterness and pride are not my most flattering attributes. Nobody likes to feel used, I guess, but I reacted rather hastily, pointing fingers and penning my grievances with threats I had no intention of following through. I stuck it out for a couple more years, then abruptly quit after my boss asked me to lie should headquarters call to check on him. This was my fault just as sure as if I'd have said, 'sure, I'll take the heat for you!' I vowed to learn from my mistakes, gave a notice (four was mandatory, but I stopped well short). I started a small 'handywoman' business. It was very popular and within a few months I had more work than I could handle.

Sue continued to manage one of the vision centers but was equally upset with the same frustrations. She eventually quit the optical business and we experienced great financial success the following two years. Working together and living together, though, were undeniably adding stress to our relationship. As long as the money was coming in, we found ourselves too busy and too tired to fight about it. But our thoughts and attitudes for one another were dimming.

Then, out of the ethers, no doubt, something very strange occurred.

Either the Universe was bored, or it was changing my direction.

It was my birthday and we were to meet up with some friends to celebrate. We planned a little get-together to watch the Steelers football game and were revving up for some of our friend's famous-to-us BBQ, no doubt a few beers and enough munchies to see us through the afternoon. First, though, we went to a local sporting goods store to look for some winter boots and a new fishing pole for our upcoming trip to Larry and Chris's place at the shore (Sue's brother and his wife).

I was looking over some rods and reels when my right leg went to sleep. *Weird*, I thought, *I didn't realize such a thing could happen when one was standing*. I couldn't seem to shake it awake. It suddenly became heavy, and this was my first sign of real worry. I tried to walk, but my right leg drug across the floor behind me. *I felt like a monster in a horror film*. It was a strain to walk, and just as I reached for a pole to steady myself, my right arm started to tingle. *Oh, no, am I having a stroke?* Sue was not in sight, and I knew I needed to get her attention. I turned to ask a cashier for help, and as I swung around, my left leg went numb...a milder tingling, but nonetheless, I began to panic, and then I saw Sue coming down the aisle toward me. The look on my face caused her to worry and walk a little faster.

"Help" I mouthed. She hurried to me and I explained my symptoms. She wanted to call an ambulance, but I declined. There was no facial drooping, I reasoned, and my speech was intact. I used her body as a crutch, and we headed for the car. The numbing continued to plague me through the day, and I tried to minimize it, but by mid-afternoon, I ended up at the emergency room. The ER ran a series of tests and admitted me. The diagnosis was slow to come, and for a couple of days I was certain it was the XP. It was my 51st birthday, after all, and the prognosis Dr. Clendenning had given me decades earlier moved to the front of my thoughts.

The hospital stay was one week, and I was diagnosed with Transverse Myelitis. While neurological decline is known to occur in some XP patients, there was no reason to believe this was related. They would eventually come to believe my myelin sheath had been attacked by a virus, a less than common diagnosis but the only one making sense. The sheath surrounding the nerves in the neck and spine was infiltrated. The ensuing damage affected my limbs but for my left arm. The neurologist prepared me for the possibility of life in a wheelchair. Physically, I could stand, but I could not feel anything but numbness in my legs, my arm, too, albeit less sensational. I declined to give his prognosis any merit. *Do you notice a pattern here?* Within two days, I was walking.

Plan B was physical therapy three days/week (I asked for 5). I would need to learn to walk again with any kind of confidence. I couldn't feel my feet touch the floor, and there were times I had to look to see if I had taken off my shoes.

Total numbness – acute neuropathy. It is something I learned to live with, and to this day, I am hard-pressed to give it much thought, but for 2 months after the incident, walking without assistance from one room to the next was a miracle. To safely maneuver steps, I had to crawl up or scoot down using my arms and my behind.

The angst of this crossed physical boundaries into other areas, most notably, my finances. I had no insurance to cover the cost of the hospital stay or treatment, there was no way my partner could handle the business on her own, and I suffered another bout of depression. Sue did her best to encourage me, but the light of hope was dwindling. As has always been my nature, I displayed courage I lacked from within, but I prayed for God to take me if I couldn't get better. I'm no martyr, but death does not concern me to the same degree as being alive and at the mercy of pity.

Some might have argued '...but, you would still be of some value'. No argument. I thoroughly believed in my value. It was strictly selfishness on my part (or laziness), and I felt I didn't have it in me to 'start over' with another challenge.

My youngest sister, Linda, came to see me at some point over the course of my hospital stay. Even now, when I think of that visit, I remember her glow. She was the light I needed to attack my next challenge. It was nothing she said, just her presence...it's the way it's always been. I heard from most of my brothers and sisters, and two of my cousins in Texas (Ricky and Carrie). My maternal aunts called. My friends showed up in numbers. My children, of course, made the trip to see me, and Sue, ever loyal and vigilant worked harder than she was sustainably capable to keep our business going.

Despite our hurdles over the years, my family has always been a soft place for me to land. I guess, technically, I am a half-sister, but my position with them has never left me feeling less than whole. It's just the way we were raised. Kim and Linda live within a couple hours' drive. Donna's home is significantly further, but we manage to see each other at least once a year. My brothers all live a distance away, and while I love them all equally, my brothers and I share less of a connection, though it pains me to admit it. I think it has been harder for them to come to terms with my sexuality, but no terms are needed for the mutual respect and love we give each other when we're together. My brother, Randy, besieged too with the heaviness of an emotionally crippling start to life, is still as close to me as either of us can tolerate, and though he and I continue to struggle with the added stress of what won't rest in our minds, he is one of the very few who understands and accepts our truth, almost as steadfastly as our brother, Terry.

Randy and I rarely mention the circumstances that forge our special relationship; we certainly never discuss it. At best, words only add to the awkwardness and uncertainty of it.

"You and me, Deb...we're always going to have a special kind of bond. You know what I'm talking about, right?" he has said on more than one occasion, the conversation always ending there, mostly because I say "Yes" and there are no other words necessary. Someday, I'm going to trick him though, and ask "Why do you say that?" Just because I'm a big sister and this is what big sisters do.

My daughter, Jessica, gave up her full-time job to help Sue handle our large client base. It wasn't the first (or the last time) she would come to our rescue. In terms of family needs, there isn't one of the kids who hasn't stepped up to help, but Jessica seemed always willing to drop what she was doing and leave nothing to stop her from helping. Tiffany managed to help by taking a day off here or there, also, and our friends, Maddie, Michele, Lynn and Annette also pitched in when they could. God provided us more blessings than challenges, for sure. After four grueling months of therapy, I was back to work half days. Only a handful of clients remained, the losses

largely due to a breakdown in equipment, but we were able to make as much as we needed to get by (barely). As for rebuilding, we felt less certain. Jessica was pregnant with her first child, and the father of the baby was unwilling to commit. The rest of us were happy to welcome another baby, but more concern came our way from the south, and we were ill-prepared for the news.

My son-in-law, Shelley's husband and an Army infantry soldier was arrested by the military for 'conduct unbecoming.' I truly wish we'd had the 'how to for' to acknowledge and properly react to his behavior from the beginning, to get him the help he needed. We didn't'; in fact, we believed in his innocence. We were woefully wrong, and time would prove us to feel partially responsible for the pain it caused other families. After collective pleas and letters written on his behalf, the charges were dropped, and he was transferred to another base where more of the same problems surfaced. He needed help. We didn't see it. The Army didn't either. To that end, my daughter, and my grandchildren, needed rescuing, too, and because of yet another brave angel and Army veteran, they are now safe and adjusting to much improved circumstances.

Sue and I had very little money, energy or confidence to attempt a re-build of the business, but we needed to do something. I was mending at impressive speed, so we took on a few more long-term jobs and things seemed to be heading in the right direction again. *All things good or bad shall pass.*

Two years after the Transverse Myelitis diagnosis, and at a regularly scheduled skin check with Dr. Tamy Buckel (resident), Dr. Liz Billingsley (attending physician, MOHs surgeon, a living angel if there ever was one) thought something not to look right. There was an area just beneath my jaw line off color and paler than surrounding areas. Even had I seen it I would have probably dismissed it as another scar. It was a miracle she even noticed it. But after the customary biopsy, it was determined to be an a-melanotic melanoma; a colorless and potentially metastatic malignancy. I have had several melanomas in my life, all black or dark brown and irregular. I was sent to a general surgeon in plastics where a wide swath around the tumor was extracted, along with a sentinel lymph node. The lymph nodes are everywhere, I'm told. They are the dumping ground for the damaged and/or unwanted cells in the body. If the sentinel node (the one closest to the tumor) is cancerous, then metastasis is a greater concern. I felt the power of prayer throughout the process, but for the first time in my life, I was feeling unusually concerned. I called on my brother Terry once again to steady me...I called on Mom and Momma, too. They must have an awful lot of influence on whatever realm they're on, because as they wheeled me down the aisle to surgery, I could feel them lift me...and cradle me toward the OR. I felt an incredible amount of love and gratitude.

A very nervous Sue, my sister Kim, and our good friend, Michele, all kept each other company in the waiting area until the surgeon appeared with the news: "Everything went well..." he said, politely, with his thick Scottish dialect. "She should be out of recovery in a couple of hours. I believe we took a wide enough area, but we should have pathology reports due back to us in three-five days, and that will verify whether it has traveled and/or to what degree the area was affected."

The wait was only three days. They did not get it all. More surgery. More wait.

I was completely unafraid for the second trip, and profoundly grateful for the team of professionals at Penn State/Hershey Medical Center. The malignancy had spread across the surface of the skin, but not deeper. The good news was a welcome respite.

"I feel good" I said, over and over again. "I have a good feeling about it. The worst of it is over."

Still, Dr. McKay said, "Chemo will most likely be recommended." I struggled with the fears of dealing with the process. I remembered my mother's challenges.

There have been many surgeries and Hershey Medical Center might be as familiar to me as it is for the people who work there. In one scheduled operation, I had some kind of correspondence with four or five dozen representatives of this institution. Doctors, surgeons, nurses, anesthetists, radiologists, phlebotomists, housekeeping, registrars, clerks, aides, social services, lab technicians and dietary...and I would consider every one of them human angels. Should you need surgery, and are nervous, it might help to remember how many professional angels are working in your behalf for the time you're there. Just saying.

The return report was good; pathology found the borders to be clear, and the sentinel node showed no sign of spreading. A follow-up in Oncology was scheduled. By the narrowest of margins, I was spared chemotherapy.

Again, I was out of work. Again, Sue and Jessica tried to fill the void. And, again, we were losing the battle of the bills. Long, busy days turned into weeks and months of frustrations. Sue's headaches returned with a vengeance. Almost daily, I needed to inject her with Imitrex. It worked about one-third of the time. I massaged pressure points, took to YouTube to learn various methods of healing, including the Emotion Code and Tapping. Our friends, Maddie and Michele used their reflexology skills to try to help ease her discomfort. We took trip after trip to doctors and chiropractors and other healers. I went to a local metaphysical store and bought some crystals. I had no idea what I was doing, but I believed the Universe would make it right...I would leave no stone unturned!

There were a lot of stones in the metaphysical store.

And then...

Sue's mother, Marion, was diagnosed with Stage 4 breast cancer.

Throughout the years, Sue and Marion struggled to find common ground. The relationship was strained, a result, I believed, of Sue's feeling of emotional neglect as a child, then again for an unwelcomed response as an 'outed' and frightened gay woman. Marion was a delightful lady to most everyone she encountered, but she had an undeniable axe to grind with her only daughter. Sue loved her mother but failed to live up to the expectations provided. They both wanted more from each other; more than each other could give.

Each craved for a better relationship, but mostly, they were at odds with one another.

The Universe began communicating with us daily.

Sue's mother was nearing the end of her journey. Sue visited her mother quite frequently and on a couple of occasions walked into her mother's room to witness Marion having secretive conversations with someone who was not there. Once, she found her playing choir director! Each time, Sue would ask "What are you doing Mom?" Each response was met with a silly grin, "Oh, nothing, just waiting for you to get here."

On a very early January morning, a hospice nurse called to tell us Marian was unresponsive. We left for the facility and arrived pre-dawn. As we exited the elevator to her floor, we were met with the noisy chirping and chatter of a couple dozen birds inside the atrium central to the waiting room. I love birds, mind you, but their piercing 'top of the morning to you' welcome was just too much to handle this sad morning.

But as I comforted Sue in the hallway and Tiffany said her private good-byes, the birds abruptly stopped. We noticed. Within seconds, Tiffany tearfully appeared from the room to tell us her Mimi was gone. Aside from the gravity of our current grief, Sue and I were both flabbergasted by the coincidence. An aide who was sweeping an area of the floor nearby explained this was not a new phenomenon. "Angels came to carry her home" she said as she swept, matter of fact, "the birds get quiet out of respect."

The following day I received a call from my Aunt Sally in California. Her sister, my beloved Aunt Patsy who'd suffered from a series of breast cancer related illnesses was in her final hours. She'd left her Florida home to visit her younger sister and became ill while there. My cousins (Aunt Patsy's daughters) were notified and two of them made the trip to be with her in her final hours. The other daughter was herself too ill to make the trip. Aunt Patsy passed peacefully, all three of her children close to her heart.

My dear Aunt Patsy often collaborated with me in 'higher' thought possibilities. She seemed to know me, at times, better than I knew myself. She encouraged me to think on a different plane...'challenged me' might be the better phrase. We didn't talk often, but often enough. Her views for the meaning of life and the beauty of what lie ahead were more like mine, and I could share them with her; at the time, only her. She entertained my thoughts and celebrated my imagination like no other. This was a devastating loss for me, and a test for my firmly held belief that she was in a more beautiful place than she'd been during her difficult life on this earth. I remember the ache and grief for what the earth lost. I remember feeling nothing short of absolute joy for heaven's gain.

Hours before my Aunt Pat took her last breath, Aunt Sally called me. She was worried for my cousin, Carrie, who had been unable to make the trip. Carrie and I have always been rather close.

Aunt Sally: "Debby, I know you have enough going on, but I don't know what to do...Carrie...I'm worried about Carrie."

"What do you mean?" I asked.

Carrie had been misdiagnosed and consequently mistreated for the harshest forms of bipolar disorder. She'd been prescribed potent, deadly amounts of mood-altering drugs. Her mother was dying, and Carrie couldn't be at her side.

In a chemically altered state of mind, Carried decided to make the trip to heaven to be with her mother. She took the pills and laid herself down for her final nap; then called the hospice nurse to leave a rather cryptic message; "Hi, this is Carrie" she said, groggily.

"Please tell my mother I love her, and I'll see her on the other side." *Some might have thought this to be innocent enough, suggesting the message referred to a 'natural born' transience in due time. I thank God every day for this hospice nurse I've never met. Another angel.*

"I don't know...I just have a bad feeling" Aunt Sally replied. "I tried to call her and there is no answer, and I tried to call Heiko (Carrie's husband) and there's no answer. It's late...and with everything going on here..."

"I will call her. I will take care of it. You go be with Aunt Pat," I said in an even tone, but I was quietly having a panic attack.

I called. No answer. I called again and left a message to call me back immediately or I was calling the police. I waited less than a minute. I dialed 9-1-1.

"9-1-1 Operator, Penbrook...what is your emergency?"

My Penbrook home is in Pennsylvania. Carrie lives in Texas.

135

"Um, yes, this is Debby Jones on S. 27ᵗʰ Street in Penbrook. I just got a call. My cousin lives in Texas. I think she is in distress. Can you call the police there and ask them to go to her home?" In the moment, I thought how ridiculous a request like this must sound and was expecting them to tell me to call information for the authorities there. It took them a second to fully understand and confirm my request, but they connected me with the proper emergency department.

Again, I hate that I don't think of what I'm going to say before I say it.

"9-1-1 operator. What is your emergency?"

"Yes, my cousin lives at (address). I think she has overdosed on her medication." I plead.

"Yes, ma'am...who am I speaking to?" said the kind officer.

"Oh, yes, my name is Debby Jones. I live in Penbrook, Pennsylvania."

"Okay, thank you Ms. Jones. So, your cousin called you to tell you she took too much medication?" He was patient.

"Oh, no, she didn't call me. My Aunt Sally called me from California. You see my Aunt's sister Pat who is also my Aunt is dying...she is with Aunt Sally...any way she is dying and my cousin Carrie who is Aunt Pat's daughter, well, she couldn't get to California to say good-bye to her mother, and she lives in your city, and anyway, she called the hospice nurse with some cryptic message about seeing her mother on the other side and the hospice nurse called my Aunt Sally where my Aunt Patsy is...she's the one that's dying, and told her about this message and my Aunt Sally tried to call Carrie, but there is no answer so she called me in Pennsylvania to ask me to try and call and I did, but there's still no answer and I don't know what to do except to call the police, and I don't have your number so I called 9-1-1 and Penbrook answered and connected me to you..." (I'm wondering if this could be the longest sentence in the Guinness Book of World Records).

"Ma'am, can you please repeat that...and speak a little slower?"

"We don't have TI-I-I-M-E!" I wail. "Please send someone to the address I gave you!"

"Ma'am," he replied softly, "I've already sent an emergency crew to the address you provided, but I need you to repeat what you told me so that I can get it all in the report."

"Oh..." I said, a little sheepishly. I repeated what I could and hung up.

A hot minute later...*SHIT!!! I forgot to tell him about the dogs!*

Carrie has four or five dogs, I think, and a monkey? Aside from her husband who we are unable to contact and a son who doesn't live close, they are her world. I don't know about their temperaments, but dogs being dogs are innately protective and I certainly don't want them shooting the dogs who are just being dogs.

I dial 9-1-1.

"9-1-1 Operator, Penbrook...what is your emergency?"

Geesh.

They found Carrie in time, and she spent a couple of months in a facility where she could be treated properly. There they discovered she wasn't bipolar at all...completely misdiagnosed. She was and is, in fact, the same funny and loving person she'd been in her early years. I don't know, of course, but I strongly suspect Aunt Patsy's introduction to a higher realm provided an open door for Carrie's correct diagnosis and treatment.

Divine Timing.

[No animals were harmed in the process.]

CHAPTER 13

It had been nearly 15 years...

...since I heard from Karen. On occasion, I would put my old friend's name into various search engines. I called the antique barn she'd once been so fond of. *No 'Karen' registered there.* I ran into a mutual acquaintance on occasion and found each of them to be equally perplexed by her disappearance. I believed her mother to have passed, merely an assumption due to her age and nothing more; I was wary of calling, either way. I looked for her on social media sites even though I doubted her to partake. It wasn't her style. She was pretty much an up front and personal, animated kind of person who would be harder to appreciate in those formats.

While surfing the internet one afternoon, though, I ran across an advertisement for a school in Hartford which left me aching (more than usual) to find her. I made some calls to no avail. I searched for old classmates...nothing. But just as I was ready to give in to the rejections, a familiar name popped up on my social media screen...could it be? I believed it to be Karen's sister. She, too, had been a classmate at Atlantic School of Hartford. It gave me just enough stamina to persist a while longer. I found her on Facebook and sent her a private message. Within a couple of days, I received a return message. It was not Karen's sister but someone who had been mistaken for her in the past. The lady also attended the same airline school as the three of us, though years later. Doing some investigating on her own, she found a clue of Sandy's whereabouts and provided it to me. I immediately sent Sandy (Karen's sister) a message. Luck?

Universe.

I didn't hear anything for a couple of weeks and had nearly forgotten I'd reached out to her. She eventually responded, telling me, sadly, Karen had passed away in 2003. I was deeply saddened by the news, but I had little time for grief. The Universe was shifting at an impressive rate. As a result, there was no short supply for peculiar events.

Within days of Marion's death, we were provided numerous clues to the existence of an afterlife. Odd and hard-to-explain events were commonplace for Sue and me. Electrical issues that caused our electrician to scratch his head. On again/off again problems with the cable (despite new wiring, connection and an 'all clear' inspection from the repairmen). A lost picture found, mysteriously enough, in plain sight of an area we'd searched at least a dozen times. Strange occurrences were multiplying, and it was a very magical and mystical time. Sue and I continued to be surprised but were never afraid. So very 'on cue' and poignant were the messages, Sue and I would deliberate in meaningful conversations around the possibilities surrounding them. The Universe was working very hard, and we were watching it, touching it, feeling it, hearing it and tasting it...yet, it went deeper than all the senses. At first, we didn't know what to do with it. Our friends and family looked at us sympathetically even as they rolled their eyes. Over time we realized what was intended for us was not necessarily intended for others, and all we needed to do was accept it. To embrace it would take a little patience and a lot of open discussion, two attributes that had been noticeably lacking in our relationship.

For a moment in time, we believed the stars had aligned.

We were right.

The Universe whispered, "I will give you what you need."

But, as time went along, we realized what we needed wasn't necessarily what we wanted.

My phone rang a little after midnight and startled me from sleep. "Hello" I answered quickly, my mind slow to catch up to my need to act as though I was awake and alert.

"Mom…" It was my son Chip, his voice cracking and muffled. Suddenly my mind was caught up and racing ahead of me in the conversation.

"Chip?" I said, anxiously. "Chip…is that you? What's wrong? Where are you?"

My son rarely called. None of my children called after nightfall unless it was an emergency.

"Mom…" in the same tone.

"Chip?" I said, "What is it, Chip? Are you okay?" I heard him breathing…*is he struggling to breathe? Is he crying?*

At this juncture I had a picture in my mind of him in a ravine, sitting upside down and trapped in a turned-over car, losing consciousness, after rolling off the side of one of West Virginia's treacherous, mountain roads. No response. "Chip" I said sharply, "where are you?"

For a second, I heard nothing. I was just about to dial 9-1-1.

"Ma-ma-ma-mom," his voice faltered. "Dad…it's Dad."

"Dad? What do you mean, Chip? What is it?"

"He's not breathing…."

Chip's girlfriend, Jess, and her mother, Colleen, a nurse who lived just a couple of blocks away, worked frantically on Gregg for several minutes till the ambulance arrived, to no avail. Gregg died of a blood clot in his heart. He had just turned 60 years old.

I called my daughters. A feeling of hopelessness consumed all of my children for weeks and months to come.

CHAPTER 14

The most powerful signal the Universe bestowed upon us...

...was the doorbell. It chimed the day we picked up Marian's urn, and brought it home. The doorbell rang, loudly and definitively. Odd, since we didn't have a doorbell. It rang just once...a resounding and reverberating 'Dong-g-g'. Startled and dazed, we simply stared at each other in disbelief. Simi, our dog, ran for the back door where Mimi typically entered. *How would she know to run to the door if we never had a doorbell?*

"Well, that's new!" I said, quizzically.

Exhausted on so many levels, but nonetheless curious, we were at a loss as to how unlikely it could be, and it took us awhile to acknowledge the source. We investigated. On the dining room wall was an old chime box once wired for sound. This was from where the sound echoed, but further inspection proved the wires to be missing...no batteries, either. Coincidentally, the buttons on the door frames had been removed during a remodel a few years before. "I think it's Mom" Sue said with a smile. "She's here to tell me she's okay."

This mysterious ring from a non-operational doorbell gave us comfort to maneuver the grieving days and weeks ahead. Hope sprang from it. Expectation. A bit of deliverance, too. It rang rarely, but it always accompanied an odd sense of worthiness and a special kind of connectedness for Sue and me. Our imagination became the natural offspring to this peculiar gift. Maybe it was something else...a clue, perhaps...whatever the intention, it was received as nothing short of a message from beyond. We'd experienced other 'goings-on' of a curious nature, but we'd reasoned them down with 'maybes' and 'buts'. There was just no way to minimize the impact of this one.

Messages of various forms appeared to us daily, often several times a day. It would be almost two years, though, before the doorbell would ring again.

Enter; December 2011. We were nearing another busy holiday season.

I had a nasty cold. It had been lingering for over a week and slow to yield. It was very early on a Saturday morning and we were at Harrisburg International Airport, saying good-bye to friends who stopped along their East Coast trip for a brief visit. Sue and I had met Jeff and Michele Milota and their two little girls a few years earlier when Michele invited me to speak at a medical conference near their home in Sacramento, California. I was not a professional speaker but experienced enough with the trials and tribulations of life with a curious health anomaly to talk to the parents of children born with the same. Their oldest daughter Aimee suffered with Xeroderma Pigmentosum, too. Though much of the diagnosis and prevention has somewhat improved, and though we each have a different subset of XP and face different challenges, we are both highly susceptible to the harmful rays of the sun. Aimee was just 10 years old. I was nearer what I hoped to be the middle of a normal lifespan. XP offers no guarantees for a long life, but I know life to be in and of itself a risky venture. So, too, do the Milotas.

It was early morning and the dark was losing its boldness. The light atop the pole in the parking lot adjacent to our urban home made a short buzzing sound and flickered just as I exited the car and rushed against the cold, damp air into the back door of our residence. Sue and I were both tired from the visit but wearier from the noisy tenaciousness of my upper respiratory infection. While Sue attempted to rest on the couch in the living room, I started up the stairs and the doorbell rang.

"Not today, Universe..." I yelled, half-heartedly, ascending to my room.

"Not today, Mom..." Sue grumbled as she slumped into the couch.

I put on my most comfortable pajama bottoms. They were a sight. Ripped and torn with a hole that exposed enough to make anyone blush, I should have disposed of them years earlier. But they were so very comfortable and more than adequate for the task at hand. I fluffed my pillow, sank into it, and before my world went dark, I caught one last peek through the window next to my bed. The sun had dawned and the light atop the pole dimmed. Sweet sleep was easy to come to me, thank goodness, and I was quick to make its acquaintance.

Too soon, though, I awakened from my nap to a loud and lengthy guttural moan. I struggled to pull myself upright on the side of my bed. My head was heavy, and my eyes out of focus. *Off kilter.* Again, I heard the repetitive groan and recognized it to be Sue. "No-o-o-o," I whispered to myself, "not another migraine – God, please, not today." Sue's struggle with painful headaches had always been considerable, for her and for anyone left to accompany her through them. In the past she would bow to insufferable torture and enslavement to these dreaded headaches. Strong as she was in so many areas of her life, she had no defense for the debilitating pain, and this day I had little energy or patience to offer in support.

"Uh-h-h-h....O-O-O-U-h-h-h" she groaned, with increasing volume and longevity. I was none too sympathetic in my response, and it appeared she was less than understanding of my condition. I forced myself from the bed and trudged downstairs, emphasizing each step with a mournful grunt of my own. *Poor me.* Once in earshot, I muttered "What's wrong, Sue" with a tone meant to sound as 'put out' as I was feeling.

"My b-a-a-ack!" she wailed "My back hurts so b-a-a-a-d"

Funny, I thought she'd apologize for making noise and send me back to bed. I was truly relieved it was her back and not her head, but also a little annoyed for the disturbance.

"Fine," I retorted, "it's probably the couch. You go upstairs, and I'll sleep down here." I was foolish to think this would be the end of it, but ever hopeful.

"No....no, no, no." she moaned on and on. "It's not that."

I supported my argument with practicality "Sue, the couch is old, and it's uncomfortable even to sit on. You probably pulled something in your back when you rolled over."

"Oh, God" she gasps "Oh, God!" My plea had no impact. She responded with more moans and whimpers.

"Do you want me to get the heating pad? Some ibuprofen?" The medicine cabinet is devoid of pain relief, but at this point I would gladly have walked to the store in my holey pajamas through the frozen slushy streets just to get away from the groaning.

"No!" was her quick and curt reply.

History shouts in my year, "you'll pay dearly for your shortness with me, Debby."

I plead (in part for my own pardon), "I don't know what to do, Sue....and I'm so sick..."

146

She said nothing for an entire 20 seconds. I hung onto every quiet one of them. She groaned and moaned again. *Will this never end?*

I sat bent over on the edge of the lounge chair, put my face in my hands and shook my head in dismal disbelief.

"How about a cup of coffee?" I muttered because I had nothing else.

She moaned louder.

Frustrated, I temperamentally barked the only words certain to make her stop. "I'm calling an ambulance!"

She moaned. She didn't argue. *Did she hear me?* I felt a tinge of panic.

"Sue? Did you hear me?" [pause] "I'm going to call an ambulance!"

"Yes" she cried. "Call 9-1-1" was her reply. It took me a moment to absorb the reality of her response. I paused, then fumbled for the phone before I looked to her again for validation.

"UHHHHHH—OOOH, Oh God, Oh God..." And, I had it.

The emergency operator asked a number of questions. A couple of moments after I hung up the phone, there was a knock at the door. *Wow, that was fast!* Not quite; it was a police officer from the Borough. At first, I was startled, but ever the polite citizen, invited him in. He took one look at Sue, sprawled out on the sofa moaning with increasing intensity, before excusing himself back outside to wait for the ambulance. *Why didn't I think of that?* The sirens indicated help was only a moment away.

The paramedics rushed in and tried their best to calm Sue. I was a bit embarrassed when she demanded morphine, hoping they didn't pay too much attention to my bed head, disheveled clothing, droopy eyelids and glassy eyes, and assume we were a couple of drug addicts. It was not lost on me that the proximity of the police officer allowed too little a head start to escape, but thank goodness, the medics didn't flinch in his direction. They mentioned something about a kidney stone and told me to meet them at Community General. I dutifully complied.

First, I changed my pants. True to its typical stubbornness, the hair would not be tamed.

The Universe whispered: Come as you are.

CHAPTER 15

Once settled in at the hospital...

...I relaxed and waited for the staff to call me back to Sue's room. I looked down to see my shoes didn't match. *'Ugh! I do not even care right now,'* but I pulled my feet back and crossed them on the floor beneath my seat just in case I cared later. I didn't have to wait long. When I entered Sue's area in the ER and ran my fingers across her forehead, I was immediately greeted with a grin and "Morphine...I love morphine." As out of sorts as I was, I couldn't deny the affect her smile always had on me. She nodded off again.

Despite the circumstances and accommodations, I was eager for the opportunity to catch a couple of brief naps in between routine visits by medical technicians. My first order of business, though, was to call Tiffany, Sue's daughter, who promised to be there soon. I called my daughter, Jessica, who would relay the news to her siblings.

The ER doctor appeared, and I couldn't see his identification tag which was okay because I would probably have butchered the pronunciation of his name anyway. Besides, he responded well enough to 'Doctor'. He ordered a CAT scan for Sue, and I braced myself for her reaction. Surprisingly, she just agreed. The morphine was to blame. Either that, or this was a Sue look-alike, and I was in the wrong room. *Sue hates CAT scans. She hates hospitals. She also hates medical bills, but mostly she hates anywhere that restricts her from smoking cigarettes.*

A little further along in the morning, Sue was in and out of consciousness, and without a hint of pain. In fact, she looked at me with glazed-over eyes to say something highly inappropriate concerning a much younger attendant who had just left the room. *This was not typical behavior for Sue. I was amused by the remark, probably because it wasn't.* An aide from radiology arrived and readied her for the gurney ride to radiology. I prayed I could get a few more moments of uninterrupted sleep, but they returned in record time. Sue said she felt better and was ready to go home. I shook my head in anticipation of a temper tantrum but was spared. Tiffany and her husband, Mike, walked in.

There was some idle chit chat amongst us, pleasantries all around, and I thought about a strong cup of coffee. No time. The ER doctor was front and center.

"Ms. Beach?" he said in pretty good English. "How are you feeling?"

"I feel great!" she replied pretty convincingly.

"Well, Ms. Beach, your scan shows you have a kidney stone," he began, then paused briefly, "and this is what is causing you so much pain." I noticed he continued to look at her chart, and not so much at her. My back straightened; my stomach suddenly queasy.

"Okay," she replied with a goofy smile. "Can you get rid of it?"

"Well, Ms. Beach, we can discuss about this, but I'm afraid you have a bigger problem." His head arose from the clipboard to give her his full attention.

Sue: "Okay-y-y-y?" She sounded thoughtful but resolute in her quest, but it was hard to take her seriously with the morphine-induced smirk on her face.

There was an unsettling inside of me. My heart paused a beat. I can't tell you how I knew what he was going to say next, but I knew...

"Ms. Beach, there is a mass on your right ovary." His demeanor lacked optimism.

For the life of me, I would not be able to explain where the next questions came from. How did I know them to be pertinent? The words rapidly escaped my mouth, and nobody was more surprised for the relevant content than me.

"How big is the mass?" I asked, "Is it less than an inch in diameter?" *Where did I read that? Why did I read it?* Before this moment, I couldn't recall anyone I'd known with ovarian cancer.

"It looks to be a about an inch" he said somberly, "perhaps a little larger than an inch."

Sue looked at me and then at Tiffany. Tiffany looked at her then me. I looked at the floor.

"We must do something soon, because this type of cancer can move very fast" offered the nice man in a white lab jacket.

Rewind! Where is the rewind button? I glanced around the room. Nobody else seemed to be looking for one. *Did they not hear what he said? Did they not understand? This can't be right! He's mistaken!*

The Universe whispers...I feel the tug of your resistance.

Sue returned her gaze to the good doctor and inquired "Okay, so what do we do now?" She quickly added, "And remember, I have no health insurance, so let's get that out of the way right now" with just a tinge of an attitude, her forefinger jutted forward pointing upward as if to say

"Hold that thought." I was familiar with this attitude. She was begging for an argument.

"Mom…" Tiffany reprimanded her mother, sternly, but softly.

Her tone was scolding, but also reassuring; the tone hard to discern in the moment. It was typical for her to have an admonishing response for her mother, though, and Sue always got an ornery kind of satisfaction from it. No one understood Sue better than her only child. Tiffany is bright, kind, and slow to react, and craftily good at reminding her mother of her priorities. Sue's daughter is as independent and forthright as her mother had hoped, and always fought for her to be. Tiffany was a better learner than most, and much better with her delivery than me…than almost anybody for that matter.

"Wh-a-a-t?" Sue teased, grinning like a Cheshire cat. "I'm just sayin'…"

The good doctor didn't hesitate. He did his homework.

"Yes, Ms. Beach, I understand. We are actually looking into your options now. Try to be patient. Wait here while we try to come up with a plan for you, Ms. Beach."

Sue let out a short, giggly grunt. "I'm not going anywhere" she said.

I grinned also, my typical response when Sue says something that she thinks funny, and nobody else reacts. I can't remember when it first happened, but no doubt it was consequent to another awkward silence. I've just always been her validation ally, her exclamation point, my way of saying "I got your back." Okay, so the morphine helped. Nevertheless, patience has never been one of Sue's super-powers, and for her to smile made me want to do the same.

Reality returned quickly, though, and my face felt hot...flushed. *Wait. What?* At this point, talking seemed a task too difficult for me to muster. I needed to do something, however...anything that would allow me to escape without leaving the room. The rest of the hospital visit was mostly a blur, but I caught bits and pieces of what needed done and the timing with which we needed to move regarding treatment. *'When the kidney stone passes, it will be extremely painful...she may notice a droplet of blood...the hospital*

will send her home with something for pain, and a 'potty' screen to catch it?' I didn't consider asking why this last part is necessary.

"It will be very painful when it passes", I heard him say once again but the room was closing in on me, toying with my thought processes.

Mostly, Sue was undaunted. *She wanted a cigarette.* "Debby, did you lock the door when you left the house?" she inquired. *She had to go to the bathroom. The cats need fed. She needed another blanket.* "So, how was your day?" she said playfully to Tiffany. Nobody was speaking of the mass on her right ovary.

Was I the only one who heard him say it?

I focused my energy on the rail side of Sue's bed. It was approximately 3 feet off the ground, which was a little high for someone of Sue's stature. A red handle, PULL HERE, arrows up and arrows down. LIFT. BRAKE. Some of the directions were in small print, but I was confident for my ability to operate the bed. *Someone, please ask me to operate the bed!* Though I found it difficult to look at Sue or Tiffany, or anyone else, I needed to do something. I wanted to pull the RED handle...I wanted to be of some use...some good. At that moment, it was the one thing I was certain I could accomplish.

Random thoughts attacked me from all angles. The rest of the room was out of focus...cloudy...surreal. *Am I dreaming?!* I blinked my eyes twice, but the scene remained the same. I shook my head, then immediately looked to see if anyone noticed.

I closed my eyes and briefly visited the day my Dad died. It was completely unlike my father to call me, yet he did...the very morning to be his last...to ask me to pick him up something from the store and bring it to him. He drew me there, unaware of his demise. Otherwise, my mother would have been alone. An early summer day that began so innocently and turned so quickly.

I swallowed hard and snapped myself back to the present. *Is Sue going to die?*

"Linda" I whispered, and I thought Sue heard me. I blinked hard and scolded myself quietly. *'Don't...Don't go there!'* I looked up quickly to Sue look at me. She grinned, then winked. I offered an abbreviated smile and lowered my head again.

I returned my focus (if I even owned such a thing in the moment) to Sue who was fussing with the edge of the white cotton blanket laid out over her middle. The effects of the morphine were no longer apparent in her eyes, but she seemed subdued. She played with the folded hem of the blanket, a nervous habit I'd witnessed over the years. Years. The number crept up on both of us. Her bright green eyes continued to be her most striking feature, but the color was paler than it once was. I wondered how much of this was due to natural progression and decline. I wondered to what degree our struggles were responsible. An unlikely pair, we most certainly were.

Aside from our value systems, there was little to compare Sue with me. On the one hand, we knew each other very well, providing a level of comfort for which we grew to expect and accept. On the other hand, we knew each other very well, providing an equal measure of futility for which we'd grown to expect and accept from one another. We'd chased the fairy tale of romance throughout our lives...and for a short time felt it so deeply, yet never again...but not forgotten...a tease of something just out of reach but always hovering...the elusive butterfly of love.

And, still, there we were.

Sue is opinionated, demanding, organized, slow to yield, and nurturing, the latter being doled out with tough love. I am personable; all over the place; uncentered, open-minded, messy, quick to yield and in need of nurturing (the latter to be doled out in tough love). We always fought harder than we loved. Still, we were always there for each other. At some point our relationship crested there. After all those years, we still battled to hold it together for the sake of one powerful moment that brought us together.

18 years of uncertainties and challenges took a toll on us, however. The blanket covering the layers of frustration, disappointment and distrust beneath the surface had unraveled. Our future together was less optimistic, our mutual dislike for our circumstances exposing every grievance we held. Apathy ate away at us. We had become woefully buried in unkept promises and hard-to-forgive annoyances; those things we were too tired to fight over but couldn't and wouldn't allow ourselves to forget. Each multiplied or compounded the cumbersome nature of the other.

After one too many failed attempts to reconcile, I asked for separation. Sue painfully resisted, and I was surprised she didn't see it coming. Soon, though, she agreed and asked if we could remain friends and house partners until something could be worked out financially. If only such a thing could be so simple. For a couple of weeks, we found it difficult to speak to each other, and we both felt horrible. There was a lot of love to look back on, but we used up an awful lot of it just getting through one storm after another. We kept swimming against the tide, and we were tired. We resented each other on so many levels. And if any one of them were valid, they all were.

For months to follow, we held it together for our friends and family, and on some level, for each other. We didn't want to hurt one another, but we couldn't stop the train of malcontent. Our children were adults, but our children, nonetheless. I didn't know if they took the breakup seriously, but they seemed somewhat dispirited by our problems, probably because they'd been front and center to most of them. They were not surprised and cautiously saddened for our announcement, but no division between them and either of us was apparent. We had four beautiful and loving grandchildren to consider, though. We were two people and one unit; never one without the other.

The circumstances and situations we hurdled over the years could test the resolve of any couple. If parenting five children and four grandchildren wasn't enough, we consistently battled one sickness after another...there were mounting financial issues. We worked as hard as any two women could, but we couldn't stop the bleeding of our bank accounts. Every day was a battle.

And, still, there we were. The Universe. It knew exactly what it was doing, but we remained ignorant of its potential.

"You should call Madeleine and Michele, Debby" she said, I believed, in part to snap me back from the self-imposed trance I slumped into. The other part, certainly, was that she wanted her friends to know. We were all like family, really. "I will take care of Mac, though" she ordered.

"Okay" was my simple and helpless reply. "Okay."

Penny and Shari? Lynn and Annette? I didn't ask, but my thoughts must have been lingering above my head and in plain view for her to read...like in comic books.

"You call Lynn and Annette; I'll call Penny and Shari" she said. No cartoon lyrics...the only thing I saw above her head was a blood pressure cuff monitor attached to tubes and a funny looking thermometer. A small television on a long mechanical arm was pushed against it. The discharge nurse was front and center; the next several minutes went by quickly. Before I was squarely aware of it, I was helping her into my car.

The trip home was mostly quiet as we let the news settle. Sue was bundled up on the passenger seat in my oversized jacket, my right hand resting just above her knee, my left hand on the steering wheel. I tried to be supportive, but I needed what little strength I had to resonate in her and then double back to me. She shivered and tightened her hand over mine. "Thanks for being with me today" she said.

Sympathetically, and at a lack for something else to say, "Of course, Sue" I responded evenly and earnestly, "Where else would I be?" It was a rhetorical question.

"Are you feeling any better?" she asked.

"I'm doing okay" I replied, "but I'm worried about you."

"Me too" she said softly. "Me too."

The grin was gone.

We pulled into the driveway; the edge of dusk...cold and damp. I looked up toward the light in the parking lot to see proof of a soft, misty rain. The wipers were on for the trip home, but this was the first I gave it any real notice. I grabbed my spare jacket from the back seat, moved quickly

157

to the other side of the car to help Sue steady herself, and we hurried for the back door. A soft humming sound appeared to be coming from the light, not unlike the one I heard earlier in the day.

The Universe whispered, but I wasn't taking messages.

CHAPTER 16

As tired as we were...

...there was no sleep in our immediate forecast. Once inside the house, I made coffee. Sue started for the recliner, then mumbled something about calling Michele, and asked if I'd seen her cigarettes. We had a 'no smoking' rule for the inside of the house, and as I was about to excuse her from obeying it, I heard the front door open. Sue was already on the front porch and I let her have this time to herself. She has smoked most of her adult life. I gave up fighting with her about it, and of course, I regretted it. Rinsing out some cups from the morning, I stood at the kitchen sink and peered out into the night again. The light was working. *'They must have already fixed it'* I thought, but then I realized it was the weekend. *Odd.* By the time the coffee had finished brewing, the pole light flashed off, then on once more. I stare at it for a moment as if to say "*I saw that! I saw that!*" But it remained on. I took a deep breath and tried to organize my thoughts, but I was distracted.

The flickering light bothers me. I won't call the Borough office or the light company...no, not even once, because I don't want to be a bother. However, I will repeatedly show up at this window overlooking the parking lot to think about it...to try and will it to be on or off...to wonder if am the only one who notices it. OCD... anxiety...both? I'm not sure, but whatever the distraction, it can render me dysfunctional for moments on end. I hear the door open again and before Sue asks me what I'm looking at, I pull myself back to my initial task.

This obsession is not my only privately held annoyance. I count... everything. As I've grown older, I have graduated to the supernatural and spiritual for explanations of my otherwise unexplainable fixations, and sometimes I wonder if OCD wouldn't be easier for me to explain. I count steps, pickets on fences, and when I can find them...sheep. I have counted the tiles on the ceiling or the floor, used my internal calculator to measure the size of each tile or floorboard, multiplied the length by the width of all the tiles, and then come up with pretty precise room measurements...all while there have been other things going on that are just too difficult for me to manage. I have calculated the height of the light pole outside this window to be 38 feet. I digress.

I poured the freshly brewed coffee. My mind was buzzing, and aching, but the symptoms of my cold seemed less oppressive. Sue was already on the phone with Michele. I grabbed my laptop to start my search for 'mass on ovary'. I heard Sue say something about calling her brother Larry. I was glad to be spared the task, not that he had given me any reason, more because I believed they needed to hear each other.

During my melanoma scare, I found it difficult to talk with the people I most loved. I needed time to properly digest the news; time to prepare myself for each reaction. I refused to answer the phone. On the third day, however, I received a message via email from my oldest daughter, Shelley:

'Hi Mom. I know you don't want to talk about it, and I respect that...I understand it...but I just need to hear your voice, Mom. That's all!'

Almost instantly, my fear recoiled. Perhaps the instincts of a mother do not fade with age, but I was equally convinced everyone has more strength than they realize. In cases such as these, love had proven to be a powerful and undeniable catalyst.

Sue needed the strength of her brother, and he needed to hear the news from her to measure his own.

After Gregg died, I'd sworn off calling people when bad news was to be delivered. I was pathetically inept. On this day, however, the phone was inevitable. There was no soft way to announce via email or text that Sue had a mass on her right ovary, and even if I discovered one, the jingles on all the phones would have commenced to serenade me to the thin edge of sanity. I updated my children and called my siblings. Calls needed to be made but aside from a few, I wasn't required to make them. A friend suggested we start a call forwarding system, another one suggests a blog. I opted for the latter.

I texted my niece, Carolyn, who was a cancer nurse. I needed information from someone who would give me the proper dose of optimism and compassion. I knew my limits. I was confident she did too. For these few phone calls, hopefulness was not necessary, but everyone expected it from me anyway. I have been the eternal optimist for most of life's little punches to the gut, but typically, I was the recipient of the punch.

This was going to be a challenge.

Sue's appointment for consultation was scheduled with Dr. Gregory Willis of Pinnacle Health's Oncology Associates. We knew someone who knew someone, and from her testimonial we pushed way any lingering 'quality of care' concerns.

People without insurance live with this fear each time they seek medical care, valid or self-imposed. Each time a patient utters the words "I have no medical insurance," it is accompanied with a silent understanding he or she may be sent packing, or worse; sent to whichever doctor is downgraded from the 'preferred pile.' Maybe it doesn't make a difference, but if we think it does, to some degree we are going to be right.

Maybe we've watched too many conspiracy-born films. 'Maybes' for me are always hopeful. 'Maybes' for Sue, generally, are not. Perception is reality to the one holding one.

Having searched every conceivable topic related to ovarian cancer, I felt ready for what the doctor might (and might not) say. With a lifetime of doctors and surgeons as my point of reference, I knew what they didn't say could be as meaningful as what they did say. My intent was to be cautious enough not to trigger doomsday reactions from my partner, and subsequently, prepare her for what the road ahead may provide; to read the doctor's eyes and stay alert for clues, to mentally record every word for the countless conversations we would hold later. Possibilities swam amok in my mind, but every challenge would be met with calm. Until, that is, a tiny voice reminded me of the greater reality not yet addressed; I was kind of a mess.

We were at the Front Street office on Tuesday morning, within 48 hours of Sue's hospital visit. The offices for 3 surgeons were located in an old historic home, smaller than most of the other mansions which mark a showy presence along the Susquehanna River, but with enough space to accommodate the 'too many' women there for treatment. Everyone was friendly and positive, including patients. It was not the pinnacle of doom, gloom and eerie quiet I expected. It was rather cheerful, even festive. Giggles and playfulness resonated from inside a door marked "Infusion Room". We passed it as we were escorted down the hall to the "Consultation Room".

Just six months prior to this event, Sue had a gynecological exam with a full panel of tests. She'd gone to Hamilton Health Center in mid-town after she experienced some vaginal bleeding. It was a 'pay according to income' facility and we were appreciative despite the long wait and antiquated equipment. The doctor was kind and reassuring. After a quick exam, he exclaimed "No worries"; "Uterine fibroids. Not life-threatening...Just come back in a year and we'll check you again. If you have any more bleeding, come sooner." No further issues occurred. While I was relieved, Sue was doubtful. I sanctimoniously reminded her of the Law of Attraction, whereby she mumbled something about me getting on her last nerve.

For the appointment, though, Sue seemed her normal self, and while she was a challenge on her best days, she seemed more concerned for Tiffany and me than for herself. This was not unusual for Sue. She carried a 'take charge' kind of resolve in such situations. "When the going gets tough, the tough get going" she'd been known to say. I shook my head. This was the familiar false bravado everyone had come to expect from Sue. I might have challenged her, but I wanted her to believe it; I needed some of it to bleed over into the rest of us.

Tiffany was with us and the wait was less than five minutes. Sue did her best to reassure us; she continued to have a little back pain but otherwise felt good. Dr. Willis entered the room with someone I believed to be a student, perhaps an intern from the local hospital. Introductions went along easy enough and Dr. Willis spoke with a factual, but positive demeanor. There was no painful concern in his eyes, no practiced words of compassion, and no beating around the bush.

"Okay, your x-rays show a mass on your right ovary. I have to assume it is cancer and will approach it accordingly. Until I get in there, we won't know anything for sure, but we don't have time to waste and wait." His face was a comforting mix of charm and forthrightness, his calm demeanor reminding me of my son, Chip. "The procedure I am going to perform is called a radical debulking" he said. "I'll cut you from here *(points to top center of his belly)* to here *(about 10-12" south)*. I will remove any cancer that I can see with my eyes. I will remove at least the one ovary, maybe both. I may also remove the uterus, if necessary. Everything will be sent to the lab and we'll go from there. Again, I will remove all the cancer I can see. Are we in agreement thus far?"

Sue nodded, and looked at me and Tiffany. We nodded in the affirmative, also.

"I don't have insurance" Sue exclaimed. She was nervous about it, of course, and found it very hard to believe they were going to proceed without payment.

"The girls up front will talk to you about all that" he said. "Not my department."

He explained a little about the entire process including pre-operative and post-operative care. He didn't know what type of cancer it was, or how quickly it might manifest. Depending on the stage,

chemotherapy and/or radiation would be prescribed. He explained her wounds from the radical procedure needed to heal before further treatment.

Sue nodded, pursed her lips in resignation, and looked at the floor. I wondered if she was counting the threads in the carpet.

He filled us in with a lot of details, and I was doing my best to keep up, but I trailed off at some points; then jumped back into the fray as my mind allowed.

He continued, "The surgery is extensive and will cause some discomfort. We will do our best to handle your pain as it comes."

The typical hospital stay is 3-5 days, and as I awakened from one of my dazes, he said something about Sue needing tests run beforehand; 'bloodwork, EKG, another CAT, a biopsy of the uterus', but the words seemed to echo as though I was in a tunnel. There was a lack of countenance on Sue's face, which made me worry about my expression. *'Do I look as dumbstruck as I feel?' 'Should I look worried or confident?' 'Do I look confused?'*

"And, stay away from the computer" said the good doctor, "at least until we have a better understanding of what we are dealing with."

"Okay-y-y..." Sue said with some hesitation, "if I have to have chemo...."

He interrupted, "Let's not get ahead of ourselves."

I liked Dr. Willis, and Sue seemed very comfortable with him. If she hand-picked a medical professional from a thousand others, he would have been the one. He was sure of himself. He wasn't a bully, but he wouldn't be bullied, which couldn't be more critical in Sue's case because her nature was to be in control. He looked a good bit younger than Sue, but his experience in these matters had been tested.

Sue asked, "Have you done a lot of these surgeries?"

He twiddled his thumbs and looked at the ceiling as though he was counting, then asserted "About a thousand."

As for the odds of beating the disease, he answered carefully, "If we get it early enough, I believe the last number I saw was 81% success rate."

Sue asked how long the procedure would be.

He replied, "It depends on what I see when I get in there...if the cancer has spread too far, I will stop the surgery immediately and close you up."

Wait! What? Close her up? To Die? I couldn't look at Sue or Tiffany or the Doctor. *Where is the bed with the red handle when I need it?*

He continued, "I won't put you through any more than necessary. If I think there's a chance we can manage it, I'll remove everything visibly effected and you'll be in surgery for at least a couple of hours; in recovery another hour or so."

Reality was checked. There was no need to read into what he wouldn't say because he spoke it.

"Okay" Sue said.

Wow was my silent contribution. Just *Wow*. I swallowed hard.

"I know the holidays are coming," he explained, "but I need to get you into surgery within a couple of weeks." Sue winced, and he saw it. "Questions?"

Sue pleaded, "Yes, our grandchildren are coming in for the holidays; I'd like to spend Christmas with them, and my birthday is January 1st. Could I..."

Before she could finish, he made it very clear. "I'll give you Christmas. I can't give you your birthday."

"Okay" she conceded while nodding her head. She seemed to be forming a thought, but I wondered if this was just her way of saying, '*You can have it your way this once – just don't get used to it.*'

"Okay," he said. "I'll have the ladies at the front desk make the arrangements for the hospital. We'll reserve your time and give you a call." His associate handed him a clip board. He took a few sheets of paper from the top and relayed them to Sue. "This information should answer most of your questions, but if you don't find the answers you're looking for, call me. My number is listed on the last page." He slapped his thighs and stood. We also stood and thanked him for talking to us. He hugged Sue. He shared the same kindness with Tiffany and me.

CHAPTER 17

The surgery...

...was performed without much of a hitch. Recovery was less than ideal, however. Sue had some difficulty with pain and then again with the medicines prescribed to make her comfortable. Once she was in the clear, Dr. Willis gathered us in a small conference room to fill us in on the details for the outcome of the radical debulking procedure. Sue's brother Larry, my daughter Shelley, a friend (Deb M.) and I were a captivated audience.

It was a brief meeting.

The cancer had metastasized. What began as a small mass on her right ovary had quickly evolved into cancer across the uterus and into the omentum, the stomach lining, and the left ovary. "In the two weeks since her first scan, the size of the mass on her right ovary grew from the size of a walnut to about the size of an orange" he said. Despite the findings, Dr. Willis felt good about her prognosis.

They'd found no indication any other organs were infiltrated by the disease. He took all he could see, the samples were sent to pathology, and she would be graded before leaving the hospital. She was stapled together, and instructions for post-op care would be discussed by the discharge nurse. He would see her within a couple of weeks to talk about chemotherapy.

Sue spent a total of just four days in the hospital and was staged as Ovarian Cancer (3-c), not as good as we'd hoped, not as bad as we feared.

As a group, we breathed a sigh of optimistic relief. Singularly, however, I began to prepare myself and the nursing staff for ramifications of 'Sue as patient'. There was a long history of Sue's non-compliant behavior, the last of which was still a freshly held memory. I began to hyperventilate for the chance of history repeating itself.

A case in history: Sue was dehydrated and as sick as I'd ever seen her. Spiking fever, vomiting, and in tremendous distress, she'd contracted a rare case of camphylobacter ju-juni, (C-coli). Before the verdict of a blood sample sent to the Center for Disease Control was returned with the diagnosis, however, all the doctors knew for sure was that two men at a local hospital had suffered the same symptoms and died. Desperate to do everything he could, the attending ER Doctor went out on a limb and gave her an IV, though the medical manuals preached against it. (Ultimately, this action saved her life.)

Sue was not a grateful patient. The waiting room for the ER was packed and there were no remaining wheelchairs. There'd been a multi-victim automobile accident, and movement by the staff was at a fevered pitch. I carried Sue from my car to the packed waiting area. No seats were available until a kindly woman stood from hers and motioned me to take it. My arms were numb, my back was strained from holding her limp body across my girth. A nurse mercifully came to my rescue and called for a gurney. She led us down a long corridor lined with people waiting to be seen and explained to us that doctors and nurses were being called in to help cover. She managed to take Sue's vitals and jot them down before she rushed to aid another patient.

Remarkably, the attending doctor was only a few minutes from seeing Sue. He'd been notified earlier in the day about a father and son who presented with the same symptoms at a local hospital. He worked earnestly and feverishly to address her, and I could tell he was concerned. Sue started in on him within minutes of becoming alert.

"I need a cigarette!" she demanded.

"You need to stay still!" he countered.

The fight was 'on'.

The good doctor motioned me out of the room to suggest I call her family. Her organs were not working to capacity. He studied me, sympathetically, as he explained the situation to me. "Her organs are failing."

My knees buckled, though, when he said "I think you should call her family. I'm not sure we can save her." Sue bellowed from behind the door "Did you HEAR me? I said I need a cigarette?" My knees and back straightened as a result of her bedeviled tone.

After a series of heated exchanges between a polite but exhausted clinician and an ungrateful Sue, he finally gave her back a little of what she was doling out, since strapping her to the bed and gagging her was illegal.

Sue as patient: "How long do you expect me to stay in here? I keep telling you I need a damned cigarette!"

Doctor as 'over it': "Trust me, ma'am, I will have you out of here as soon as I can..." followed by "...Actually, where I'm going right now is to find a priest...so he can perform an exorcism."

He left the room and Sue struggled for a moment to compose herself from his scolding; then retorted, almost begrudgingly, "I like him."

Thanks to some pretty serious pain management medicines, we were mostly spared of Sue's disagreeable nature. To the contrary, she was very well well-behaved, humble, and gracious. Gratefully, and as an advantage, some of these drugs would go home with us. As an added bonus, cigarette smoking would be a habit she would have to live without. Apparently, nicotine and chemotherapy do not mix.

Keeping everyone up to date with Sue's battle was made easier through a patient's blog called *'Caring Bridge'*. This allowed her to rest in lieu of the phone ringing. It also permitted me to stay sane for the same. I concluded my first post-op blog before she got home and continued to update as often as time permitted...or when there was something to report. The first year of her new normal left little time for me to do anything but keep up. Her condition (mood and sickness) could change without warning....and did...often.

The slow 'ups' and the multiplying 'downs' were beginning to materialize, and there was no end in sight. Sue would sport a good day, then two or three bad ones, and the chemotherapy treatments hadn't even started. She wanted to eat, but she was unable to move her bowels. Stool softener, Milk of Magnesia, prune juice. Her colon was in extreme distress. Pain was persistent but not intense. She complained of 'electrical shock-like pain' in her abdomen. Restful sleep was elusive. She might doze off in the lounge chair from time to time but lying flat proved too uncomfortable for any length of time.

Chemotherapy started in March. She was eager to get started. I understood. When cancer pledges an assault on the body, its intention isn't temporary. It devours you. It imposes fear and exposes vulnerability, steals identities and mocks the body's ability to fight back. It steals your hair and pillages your dignity. Once you've accepted those truths, you'll suffer the greatest of extremes to rid yourself of it. You'll go at it again and again just to hang on to the best of what remains…your heart and your soul.

Three weeks after her first infusion, Sue was in the shower and I was on the phone with Kelsey, my youngest daughter; a ray of sunshine through the darkest of days. We'd barely started our conversation when Sue yelled from the shower in the adjoining room, and the sheer volume of her voice caused me to panic.

"Kelsey, I have to go" I said, hurriedly and hung up the phone. "What is it, Sue?" I yelled back as I jumped from the chair and barged through the bathroom door.

She stood naked and shivering in the tub staring at a handful of her hair. I grabbed a towel to steady her. Strands of brown hair against the white porcelain proved to be more ominous than what we'd prepared for. There were no words between us. I stepped into the tub and hugged her stiffened body. It took a moment, but she hugged me back.

Sue's chemotherapy schedule consisted of three rounds of once a week for three weeks 'on' and then one week 'off' and repeat. This translated to just under six months of treatments. The infusions were intravenously injected through a permanent port attached near the front clavicle. She complained more for the port than the chemo. Before the cocktail of carboplatin and paclitaxel were inoculated, she was given Benadryl and steroids to ward off allergic reactions to the drugs and to assist the chemicals in destroying cancer cells. She was also given anti-nausea medication, both on-site, intravenously, and in pill form for her non-infusion days.

Within the first three months, her cancer markers (CA-125) dropped considerably, then held steady, rarely fluctuating at all. The second three months saw them drop to a very optimistic 13 (down from nearly 300).

This was very good, but Dr. Willis thought it best to stay aggressive against the disease and suggested she continue the regimen for six more months. She didn't think twice and agreed. Sue's numbers were always considerably lower than other women in her little corner of the chemo room, theirs peaking in the hundreds of thousands.

The medical professionals warned us about lending too much importance to the CA-125 markers, but it was difficult to ignore them, probably because they continued to test for and report on them. They were very important to us because it was the only way we knew to measure her status, though other factors remained equally critical to the success of treatment. The ideal CA-125 measure might have been zero, but other conditions could have caused it to rise also, with no indication of cancer at all.

Within one week of her chemotherapy start, Sue made friends. Five women, once strangers, were soon connected by the same fate. Sue, Diana, Kelly, Maryann, and Mary formed a little band of warriors who traded encouraging words and poked fun at each other throughout their ordeal. Their mantra was simple; '*Believe*'. The undisputed leader of the group was Diana, a young mother with stage 4 ovarian cancer. Diana's attitude and inspiration kept them all from falling through the thin ice of surrender with her 'old soul' wit and compassionate-laced humor. She'd battled the disease before Sue's arrival, courageously shouldering her ups and downs with grace much like a Princess who'd shared her name. Without a doubt, Sue was second to the throne.

None of their victories, losses or day-to-day musings would have been possible, however, but for the nurses and staff who tended to them...heartened them, and dare I say, loved them through the many challenges and ordeals they traveled. Kudos to the women on the front lines of the Pinnacle Health's Ortenzio Women's Cancer Center; Barb,

Sue, Alyssa, Amy, Deanna, Laurie, Lisa, Nicole, Kim, Robin and a host of others, showed up every single day to temper any negative feelings relative to the challenges of these women. They were all in it together.

A sign just inside the doors to the infusion room summed up the general attitude there:

THERE ARE NO VICTIMS HERE: ONLY WARRIORS

After nearly twelve months of chemo, Sue entered remission, but was cautioned for another round (typical, we were told). She had a remarkably good year, though, highlighted by a playful schedule twenty years in the making. We went on a family cruise with most of the kids accompanying us. Sue's oldest friend, Cindy MacDonald (Mac, for short) and her partner, Ruth, made the trip as well. Mostly, we had a good time, but as it always was with us, there was equal time devoted to arguing. Sue was a bit of a curmudgeon, but the cancer and the chemo had little to do with it. She was being who she was, and I was just being me. Sue had always played the sensible, practical, discerning adult. I might have been a candidate for the kiddie pool. Had the cruise lasted a day longer, I may have been thrown overboard.

Within a few months of disembarking the ship, though, we were already planning our next family vacation. This was precisely when the wheel of fate started to turn. I noticed a change in both of us...she was softer...I took a more serious tone.

Dream. I am alone in the back car of a roller coaster. The ride never reaches the top. It just keeps climbing with anticipation...so too, does my heart rate. As we near the apex, I begin to panic and shake. One by one, the cars ahead of me jump the tracks and plummet to the earth below. I am locked in the car. My breathing is heavy and all I can do is hold on, but as I clench the iron railing, the hold is pliable and slick, my hands cramping with intensity. It kept moving away from me and the screeching of the rails sounded a lot like...

Poor cat. I wasn't certain which feline I'd temporarily latched onto, not that it mattered. The ensuing chaos of the event managed to send the entire house into a frenzy. My dream scream, comparable to high frequency humming, along with the ensuing thunder of 12 additional paws and two feet could be heard somewhere between my muddled slumber and sanity. I felt Sue's hand gently rub my upper arm, "It's okay, Debby, it's just a dream..."

One of the women succumbed to the disease. Kelly was an illness-embattled woman I would guess to be around 50. She'd suffered with stage 4 breast cancer. Sue remained upbeat, though, willing to reach out to other patients and encourage them. An even more devastating blow, though, was a few short months away. Sue's two-year chemo buddy and fellow warrior, Diana, died. She was just 44 years old and had been a strong presence for Sue.

Sue struggled to keep her hope and composure but was reminded by Diana's husband how important it was for her to keep up the fight in Diana's memory. Within a few months, though, another in the circle left too soon. And then there remained two; Sue and Mary from the original group, left to soldier on. Sue's strength was waning. I sensed it. Mary sensed it. Despite Sue's comical, cantankerous and stubbornness nature, the nurses began to sense it too.

Time went by with lightning speed but included long days and sleepless nights. Sue continued to suffer pain and cancer-related health issues. Low white blood cell counts. Infections in the port site. Fevers. Ruptured hernia. Once her numbers were in safe range, more surgery was performed to repair the latter. The pain subsided for a bit and for the briefest of time, we blinked: the cancer had progressed. More chemo.

Radiation. Her white count was dangerously low, once again, and she was admitted to West Shore Regional Hospital.

Near the end of the third year of her battle, Sue was met with an increasing number of hospital stays due to low white blood cell counts. For the most part, she took them in stride. Me? Not so much. When she was home and able, we visited friends, but rarely saw the door open in our direction. People needed to be in their comfort zones throughout Sue's illness, and while she understood this quirky truth, I was angered by it. Didn't they understand the need for our comfort zones to be occupied with love, and laughter (and my denial) too? My demeanor didn't get any better for a while.

For over three years, Sue pushed back with great muster at this cruel and unyielding disease. At some point, and as a surprise to me, Sue conceded her battle would be lost, though her unparalleled ability to dole out more than she took held the rest of us, her army of cheerleaders, to believe she would be victorious. She was as fierce a fighter as there was...formidable in every area of life well after the diagnosis.

So, it was no easy pill for me to swallow when she called from the hospital to tell me she had spoken with Dr. Willis and decided to go on hospice.

WHAT?

CHAPTER 18

It was the weekend of Palm Sunday...

...and Simi, my beloved, loyal canine laid helplessly in her bed across the room. She was panting noticeably and out of sorts. I called her to go outside with me, but she struggled to get out of her bed, then collapsed. Calmly, as though I was coaxing a frightened child, I called to her again. The look she offered me showed her intention to obey...but her body would not let her. My eyes welled...my feet did not move...my heart paused...*'no, God, no!'*

Sue, home from another lengthy hospital stay sat on the recliner, staring out the window at a hanging basket of freshly blossomed purple pansies. Her skin was pale, her green eyes insipidly flushed, her once thick brown hair white and thinning. She saw Simi struggle, and mumbled something to her I couldn't discern. She called for me, "Debby, something is wrong with Simi." There was no sympathy in her tone. No emotion at all. In this moment a reckoning was beginning to wrestle with truth, my faith and my consciousness. *Acceptance.* I had no pain, but it was difficult for me to breathe. I felt the heaviness of hopelessness settle within me and I was unable to be angry for Sue's inability to feel for our sweet dog...or to offer me reassurance. Simi's eyes held sadness. Sue's eyes were empty. For perhaps for the first time in my life, I felt truly alone.

The following day, our friend, Lynn, went with me to take Simi on her final ride. My beautiful, sweet Simi fell asleep in my arms for the last time but burst out of the room before she took her last breath. I couldn't finish, but I was with someone who could...and did.

I sobbed...not for the life that left Simi...not for the life leaving Sue...but for the life that was leaving me.

Into the valley of the shadow of death.

The Hospice team arrived as directed the day before Sue would leave the hospital. A bed and oxygen tanks were provided. They brought introduction packets, instructions, schedules and a box for the refrigerator that read "FOR EMERGENCY ONLY" and "KEEP REFRIGERATED". Her care nurse told me what to expect. I didn't want to know what was in the box. I wanted to tell her not to bother coming back, too, but I offered her cookies instead. While decorating a plate with them, I recalled one of Sue's favorite sayings; "if you don't want them to come back, don't feed them." I smiled.

They were scheduled to come once a week until the need became greater. They would hire a caregiver to come twice a week to bathe her and do some light cleaning. This allowed me time to run errands. I hadn't worked in weeks and had no idea how we would pay our bills. Frankly, I didn't care, but our friends did what they could to help. They came to our rescue with food and donations to help us make our house and utility payments.

'When the going gets tough, the tough get going', but I wasn't feeling tough at all. I was feeling sad for Sue's decision to leave, but I was in a zombie state for much of it. When able to muster an intelligible thought, it was still extreme. I wished it to be a bad dream. I wished I had run away when I had the chance. I wished it would all be over. Somewhere inside the gloom and doom of our situation, though, I held onto the thought that the Universe would intercede and make her well. I found myself trying to bribe the nurse and the caregiver with fresh cookies with

180

each visit, simply because I thought they had the power to change the situation.

I assaulted them with her accomplishments as though it would make a difference. 'Sue ate a little bit of ice cream,' 'she asked for coffee,' 'walked to and from the bed to the kitchen with little assistance,' 'giggled at the antics on the ELLEN show,' and she was sweet one minute and contesting the next, which meant she was the same 'alive-and-well-and-giving-me-fits-Sue' she's always been...and were they, maybe, wrong to be there?. I wanted to tell them that the morphine was just making matters worse: that it sometimes made her combative. It doesn't let her sleep, and it causes her to see people that aren't there, and to hear voices that none of the rest of us hear. I looked for every conceivable glimmer of light that remained and reported back to them. Couldn't the doctors be wrong?

Over and over, they would make the smallest of arguments against my plea. I was powerless. It appeared to me they practiced their responses over and over. Day after day, death after death.

Within two weeks of Sue on hospice, she became fevered and very ill. It was late evening. Her pain was heightened. I called Hospice who immediately paged a nurse. Within minutes of her arrival, the nurse summoned Dr. Willis who ordered Sue to go to the ER. She was admitted, rather hurriedly, and before the end of her first day there, she slipped in and out of consciousness. The attending nurse suggested I call anyone who wished to say good-bye. I called her daughter, her brother, my children and grandchildren, most of them having to travel long distances. Within a few hours, there were fifteen bodies sleeping on matts and pull-out chairs waiting vigil through the night. We took turns sitting awake by her side waiting for any sign and hoping against hope she would pull through.

She did.

For the next four days, we were given the same forecast...four times.

Not so fast.

She was discharged and back to home hospice on the fifth day, barely the same person we'd admitted.

I was barely the same person who'd taken her there.

Her condition rapidly progressed, nonetheless. It was difficult to know for sure if it was the morphine or if the cancer had traveled to her brain.

My daughter Shelley requested an indefinite leave of absence from her job at St. Clair Hospital in Pittsburgh to help me take care of Sue. The teenager who once gave us fits, now gave us support; the very best of herself. All of our children and their partners took turns tending to daily needs of our situation. They did an admirable job, given neither Sue nor I were coping as well as we'd hoped. Every day held new challenges.

Sue had a difficult time staying comfortable in one spot and would often confuse one of us for someone from her past. *Talk about a gut punch.* We moved her from bed to chair to couch and back to bed dozens of times every day. At times, she became physical, and at other times, frustrated or detached. She had everyone's attention for all of it, though, and I was grateful to have our family there.

On one occasion, she jumped from her bed and attacked me with such force, we both went to the floor. The intravenous feed line was pulled taut and I was terrified she would pull it out. To keep her from hurting herself (or us), Shelley and I kept her on the floor until the cavalry arrived. To the rescue, our son-in-law, Mike, rushed to help; he gently scooped her up like a child. He sat her on the bedside and spoke softly to her "What's going on Mom?"

Her eyes were empty, a leftover tear under her left eye.

182

She simply said, "Hi Mike" and nothing more. But within a couple minutes she called to me. Her eyes were sad, and I was trembling from the inside out, but she puckered her lips as an invitation to put whatever happened to an end. I kissed her and she said, "I love you."

"I love you, too, Sue" was my apologetic reply, but my heart plunged. It would take the better part of a year for it to find its proper place again.

I went through a range of emotions, anger among them. I cursed the Universe for letting me down yet resisted every attempt for it to provide me assistance. It persisted, though, and used Sue herself as its muse. The Universe knew I couldn't say 'no' to her.

For the umpteenth time, we steadied Sue from the bed and into the lounge chair. She was particularly annoyed with me. Apparently, I hadn't been quick enough to acquiesce. Still, I remained patient with her...hopeful, too. "Sue, I just made some soft cookies...would you like to try one?"

"No" she answered, a strange look on her face.

She stared right past me.

"Hey...Debby" she commanded "don't let him in!"

"What?" I asked, baffled. "Who?"

"That man" she said, matter-of-factly, and pointed at the door adjacent to where Shelley sat. Of course, I saw no one. Curious as to the nature of this illusion, I asked her a couple more questions.

"Sue" I said softly as I knelt beside her, "is the man scaring you?" followed by "Is he a bad man or a good man?"

"He's neither" Sue said firmly. "But he wants me to go with him and I'm just not ready."

Followed by "Don't let him in!"

"Okay" I said "Okay, he is not allowed in...not today." For affect, I shook my finger at the empty space in front of the door, "Kind sir, you are not welcome here today...no, not today, sir."

She winked at me and said, "Thank you."

I winked to the Universe and mouthed, 'Thank You'.

I was growing cranky with hospice. The women were wonderful and kind, but they were interfering with my pity party. I complained to everyone except hospice, of course. They got smiles and cookies...and some pretty amazing briefings.

"Something very interesting happened..." I said to Nurse Cathy on more than one occasion. Interesting indeed.

The television was on...Sue seemed comforted by it even if she couldn't comprehend what was happening. While I typed up the daily blog, Shelley sat in the lounge chair for one of the rare moments of peace offered from Sue's area of the room. It was a very warm and still April afternoon and we'd opened one of the windows to let in some fresh air.

I was in the kitchen when I heard her. Shelley, not Sue.

"Su-u-u-u-e!!??" she roared. I turned on my heel fearing the worst, only to see Shelley rise from her chair and turn to stare at the wall behind her. "Sue, what was that?"

As I hurried into the room, I saw Sue with the orneriest of looks on her face, staring at an embroidered wall hanging given to us by her mother. Shelley's eyes were wide with fright.

"What happened?" I said, startled by both of their expressions. "What?"

Shelley did not look at me. She looked squarely at Sue. "Sue!" she demanded, a little unnerved, "What was that?"

Just then, the embroidered wall ornament flapped against the wall; Sue's face still wreaking of mischief. "Well," she said with a half giggle, "some people think it's..." her eyes closed, and she was out. Not dead, as we first thought, but out.

"Sue?" Shelley said, sternly but inquisitively; playfully. "You did not just go to sleep without telling me what that was!" We traded looks of complete surprise, Shelley's with a hint of disbelief; mine with a tinge of 'the Universe is at it again'.

As the days turned into weeks, Sue's mind took a sharp turn into the deep past on occasion, then into the deep beyond. Curiously, late on a Sunday evening;

"Debby-y-y!" she yelled on the edge of hysteria. "The cat...the cat!!"

I reacted instantly, "What is it, Sue?" We had three young cats...all sleeping soundly near the window.

Sue was crying; "It got hit by a car". She was inconsolable.

"No" I said sympathetically, "No, babe...you've just had a bad dream."

"No!" she insisted "No, I saw it...the cat got hit by a car and it's dead!" She was crying and inconsolable.

I grabbed some tissues for her to wipe her face and soothed her as much as I was able. I ran to both doors and looked up and down the streets. Shelley and Jessica hurried to pick up the cats to offer proof of their safety. I wiped her head and held her close. "See? They're all here...they're all okay."

"I saw it Debby. I saw it." She wiped her eyes and then she was asleep.

185

The following day, her niece, Margie planned a visit. Margie lives in Maryland, not far from Baltimore and has always had a special place in Sue's heart. A few minutes before she arrived, Sue woke from a sound sleep, sat up in bed and declared "Margie's here. She just pulled in the driveway."

Sue's position was in the front room and the driveway is in the back of the house.

"No, babe" I replied apologetically "not yet..."

She argued. "Yes she is...I saw her pull in."

I tried to placate her. I was trying to think of what I could say to subtly change the direction of the conversation when Margie entered the back door.

Sue knew things we didn't know. She spoke of them, even if we found it hard to believe her. I could elaborate on each, but the result was always the same...she saw things, heard things, knew things the rest of us didn't. A boy was playing with toys under her bed and was going to get hurt, yet no children were present. A crow watched her from atop the light pole as if it wanted something from her, but from where she sat, the light pole wasn't visible. (I saw the crow on a number of occasions). According to Sue, a house was on fire three blocks over, and 10 minutes before we heard any sirens. To seal the truth for the things she shouldn't have known, she exclaimed as a matter of fact, "and if you want that light on the pole fixed, you'll need to call the borough office."

She'd have pain and we'd up the morphine to calm her. But, each and every time, my anxiety and sense of futility fostered the concerns for a motive. *Was I killing her with the morphine?* Silly, but it bothered me.

I put her in the chair to help with the stiffness and pain in her lower back. I took my eyes off of her for less than a minute. She stood, then crashed face-first on the floor. Blood gushed from her nose. I didn't want hospice there, but I couldn't keep her safe. Through it all, an emergency kit sat unused in our refrigerator. *I wondered if it might be for me.*

We tried our best to keep her comfortable, but she complained about the bed. We borrowed a single mattress and lay it on the floor adjacent to the couch. She was less likely to jump up or get hurt falling out of the hospice cot. Days turned into weeks and Sue gradually became less talkative, less animated, and less awake. Gaunt and weak, she hadn't eaten a single bite in 12 days. Still, though, we saw some of the Universe's finest displays, leaving us to wonder, playfully and peacefully, beyond the grief.

The cats who had been a source of salvation and calm, suddenly became antsy. Two of the three found refuge under the metal framed hospice bed, while Lightning, the largest of the trio began jumping and running about the room, swatting at the air and screeching meows. Shelley thought her antics to be comical and video-taped the event. Upon replay, we found the cat was chasing tiny balls of light across the room and around Sue's body.

Orbs.

On my May 5th blog, I wrote just two words: *She's gone.*

May 5th, the anniversary of Terry's death.

For three and a half years I sometimes allowed myself to accept the notion of her impending death, but the actual experience was nothing like I imagined. It was hollow, not spiritual. The air was still. There was no movement in the room at all, no tunneled light divinely jutting from a distant source, no unexplained soft breeze or passing prickle of the hairs on my neck. The pain shifted sharply from her to me, misplaced…displaced and directionally intentional, and I felt it deeply, but I could not touch it as it entered, nor soften its thrust.

I watched as life left her body and imagined her spirit rising from its earthly shell to hover above us.

Shelley cradled her head in her arms and gently stroked her cheeks. "Oh, Sue," she said softly, "we love you, Sue" she said in resignation.

I knelt beside Sue, comforting her during her transition to another place. *Comforting?* Noble, but equally ridiculous in comparison. She was transitioning on her own. I felt helpless…. dazed, and weirdly, wretchedly detached from my emotions as though it was me who left my body. *'Quit making this about you, Debby!'* I couldn't help but see her chastising grin in my mind's eye, as my eyes began to swell. I was not as scared as unsure, though, and I willed myself to move when the only reason to do so was to prove to myself I could.

Shelley did her best to comfort me with a slight shake of her head and a sympathetic whisper, "she's gone, Mom." She attempted a reassuring smile to comfort me, while she held Sue in her arms, caressing her stepmother's head and holding back the tears we both knew lie willfully trapped beneath an emotionally raw surface. There was one more breath left in Sue, though, accompanied by a relinquishing sigh. Her head tilted with gravity. Gone. *She's gone.*

I gasped, slightly, but I did not cry. It was as though I incurred my obligation to wear the grief with some similitude of dignity. Still, I never felt more defeated. I could not escape it, nor could I reject it. Death won and exposed my every doubt…my every fear.

It wasn't about the loss so much as the manner. No, it was that, too, in equal amounts. It was loving her with all I had and knowing I couldn't save her; her knowing I couldn't. She fought hard. She wanted to beat this. She didn't want to leave.

This was not the way I envisioned it. Not at all. This. This thing called death.

There is no way to prepare for such a loss. It is impossible to embrace any logic that suffering demands...no way to imagine the depths to which the heart and soul are capable of plunging. I had relied on the power of words my entire life, and there were none to accurately describe it.

I knelt beside her lifeless form. "Fly with the angels, Sue...soar!" I whispered softly, but the words lacked convincing. *To her? To me? Can you hear me, Sue?* My heart fell like a knot dropped into my stomach and stayed there until my lungs, starving for air, demanded its return. I fixed my stare on her, afraid to blink for fear that I would miss her reply. The overwhelming sadness was not that she was gone, but that she was gone without me. I'd had over three years to address the idea of life without Sue, and it wasn't enough. The diagnosis for Sue had been grim. The diagnosis for me; denial. In a very spiritual, electric way, I quietly reassured myself that our connection could not be broken. *Could it?*

The grim vigil was over, or at least the direction shifted. Sue's face transformed into one I used to know so well. Death was beautiful on her. Her skin was soft and flawless, and as breathtaking as the day we met, the lines tugging at her eyes and temples for the past 78 months mystically, suddenly disappeared. I kissed her forehead and drew back. The response, surreal as it was, was no response at all. I heard a ticking of the dining room clock and realized the mortality of the moment; the fleeting existence of life.

She was gone.

I felt incidentally and trivially small, impaired and insignificant, an audience to what was left of my own life; a synergetic consequence of two minus only the physical faculties that remained of one.

Our love was fluid, the elements undetectable and difficult to divide, like hydrogen and oxygen. Comparable to the complexities of the ocean and of oneness; swelling, cresting, ebbing and flowing; at times turbulent, but always coiling back upon hitting the shore...bubbling, foaming and splashing at the borders, evaporating with warmth, then spilling back with the clash of too much heat and stiffening cold. The truest and rawest emotion: never still and moving like water always does...at times subtle, at times raging.

Sue's diagnosis had tested us, but 'we' were confident. Our hopes and our doubts formed a tumultuous and telling river of agonizing uncertainty, that rose with slapping sounds that mirrored the accumulation of each into the last stillness. *He stands with me beside the still waters*, but I felt no presence at all. In the end, I felt only absence.

I moved to the side porch step to feel a cold rush of air slap my face. The people from the funeral home were there, the black van to transport her still running outside; the nurse on his way with a death certificate.

A light flicked on across the street. My neighbor, Vivian, walked hurriedly towards me. She heard the van and saw me; knowing the hour was well passed my personal curfew, she assumed the worst.

"Debby" she said softly, as she entered the side gate.

"Viv..." I acknowledged, before I lowered my head into my hands.

"I'm so sorry, Deb" she said.

"Thank you" I replied.

We sat for a couple of minutes. No words.

190

"You know" she said, "my Maya died last week."

Maya was Viv's beloved cat and had I not quickly related it to one of Sue's last declarations, I might have felt it an insensitive comparison.

"Maya?" I said, my interest peaked. "How...?"

Before I could finish, she said. "Yes, she was hit by a car last Tuesday...over in the alley behind Boas St."

My mouth flew open.

She continued, a bit bewildered by my reaction; "I was just thinking," she continued, perplexed, "much as she loved Maya...well, she'll have Maya there with her."

I blurted out a giggle, then laughed, unabashed. Viv was only slightly taken aback. She put her hand on my shoulder. I sat at the garden's edge and giggled until I cried, and then I couldn't stop crying.

CHAPTER 19

The grandchildren arrived from WV…

…and I felt better for their presence, convinced I had some super-maternal gift to help them cope with their loss, perhaps the largest they'd dealt with in their young lives. While each had experienced the sadness accompanying loss with various family members, mixed feelings emerged, along with some hard questions; *'Why?' and 'What happens next?'*

Most of the time, our responses lack convincing, at least that's been my experience, in large part because kids are told so many different things, and partly because we've strangled their imagination, by insisting 'real' is what can only be seen, touched, heard, etc. "Heaven?" "Where in the sky?" "God?" which turns into "If he loves us so much, why…?" and "If he's so powerful, why…?"

We tell them their loved ones have gone to heaven, and they're pain-free and happy, when they've associated happiness with their loved ones… here. And, we imply death merely to be a sad but beautiful part of life; that we all will eventually die and go live in heaven and be together again someday (which makes them wonder why we didn't all just stay there to begin with). Do we even consider they can hardly wait for a day of school to dismiss, let alone imagine a lifetime before they see their loved ones again?

Then they watch us cry and mope around inconsolably for weeks. We are terrible liars, the lot of us.

Sue's death hit the kids hard. Though they'd been warned, it is incomprehensible for a child to take the time to consider loss until it happens, and then it happens dramatically. But it was particularly devastating for our 16-year-old. Peyton is our first grandchild and only slightly younger than our youngest child, Chip. Sue and I had often given thought to Peyton being the first child from birth we shared, but without argument, she was "Nanny's girl". And, it was another one of those hard-to-explain, and not-so-ordinary circumstances which eternally tied the two of them together, when Peyton was just a few weeks old.

The phone rang and I answered.

"Mom!" The frustration in Shelley's voice was evident

"Yes, Shelley?" I replied, sensing her urgency, "Is something wrong?"

"I just can't do anything with her! I don't know what to do—she just won't stop crying!" she was hysterical; frantic.

"Okay, you just need to calm down a little, babe" I reasoned. "She senses your anxiousness."

"Mom!" she said impatiently and with a little tinge of said anxiousness.

"I can't....I just can't." Her her voice cracked, and I was reminded of the same kind of panic I experienced nearly 20 years earlier (when I called my mother).

"Okay, okay" I said in my super-mom, super-calm voice. "Why don't you bring her over?"

I was barely off the phone when I heard her enter the apartment door, the baby screaming and Shelley clamoring anxiously up the steps.

Instinctively, I took the baby and continued with the super-grandma, super-calm voice, to no avail. I tried everything, while Sue increased the volume on the television to drown out the sounds of the surrounding chaos. Sue had been not so eager to enter the realm of grandmother-hood. The volume button on the remote control was just another tool she'd found to punctuate her dismay; our unwed daughter had gone and gotten herself pregnant. Sue was not going to be party to it. (Sigh).

But, after about 15 minutes of a screaming baby, a hysterical mother, and a not-so-super-calm grandmother, she turned off the TV, uttered "Jesus Christ", jumped to her feet, stomped in our direction and demanded "Give her to me!"

Before we could think to save the baby, we saved ourselves and practically threw the infant at her. Abruptly, Peyton lay silent, chest-to-chest with Sue as she laid down on the couch. One heart to another.

They've been that way ever since. Divine intervention.

While the three younger kids somewhat feared their stern grandmother, Peyton challenged her. It was not uncommon for Sue to be infuriated with her one minute and praise her the next. Temperamentally at odds with one another, Sue could be both angry and proud of her at the same time. It drove the rest of us nuts. Oh, the times we've jumped to react to one of Sue's unreachable demands or Peyton's less than compliant responses...hearts racing...to find them cuddled up on the couch together, laughing and tickling one another before we could travel the quickest road to a reasonable outcome.

The boys, Elijah (13) and Caiden (9), offered a certain element of balance to the raucous, dramatic, and high-maintenance energy of their female counterparts, Peyton and Jaycee (7). *And some people say there is no Grand Plan.* The boys were calmer, or perhaps wiser, or both. Whatever the concoction that made their young dispositions what they were, they kept us out of the liquor cabinet once we survived a visit with either of the girls.

'Nanny' was a constant in their lives, and this was what they knew; continuity, consistency, love. Some people didn't understand it; "But you are their real grandmother, right?"

This lack of understanding couldn't change what our little family knew to be true about love. *Blood is thicker than water, but it is not thicker than love.* The grandchildren were biologically mine, but they never understood the difference. It didn't matter to them, nor did it matter to us, but it mattered to others, who qualified as being those for whom it shouldn't have mattered! Our not-so-typical lifestyle was of little consequence to the way we identified ourselves, but family was everything to the kids. Sue was their 'Nanny'. I was their 'Momma'. Our five children were 'ours' though we didn't share the same DNA markers.

We identified as family because we were the truest definition of it.

May 7, 2015. I awakened early; everyone still asleep. Sue was gone but the heaviness in my chest seemed intent on resting there for an eternity. I quietly stepped over sleeping beauties scattered about the living room, careful not to arouse them. It had been a rough 36 hours for all. I grabbed my hat and gloves, put on my long-sleeved garden shirt, and headed for the 48' X 3' garden-scape terrace bordering our yard at the sidewalk.

Tears were slow to manifest but a feeling of betrayal kept them at bay. I'd held fast to the notion her suffering had gone too far and prayed for her death in those final days. It was, in this way, another burden for me to reconcile. *Be careful what you wish for.* I convinced myself that letting go of my emotions would be to surrender, and if I surrendered, I would tear away the remaining threads of my sanity...everything swelling inside of me throughout the ordeal waited for a cue to release and I had a houseful of reasons to keep my composure.

I carefully positioned myself to avoid the sun and greet an otherwise typical, mid-Spring kind of day.

Our little garden had always been my refuge. Between a couple of grass shrubs, a long strip of dirt served as foundation for my annual display of decorative flowers and vegetables for nearly two decades. Perennials, none so beautiful as the roses, sprouted early this spring, and a small patch of organic soil was barren, begging inclusiveness. My first rose was planted in memory of my grandmother, the second for my mother, the third for Sue's mother, then my Aunt Pat, my infant cousin Jordan Tucker, and my cousin Roger Alan. Family is very precious to me, and it was my little way of honoring those who have left me behind. I purchased Sue's yellow flower, yesterday, the morning after she drew her last breath.

I have my own little fantasy for this ritual. For as long as the flowers stay in my garden, the spirits of those who they memorialize will maintain them; they do a fine job! Should the flower die, my heart pauses a beat but only for a moment. Once the flower stops flourishing here, its spirit has simply moved on to another garden that needs more care, to another family in need of their love and attention. It may sound far-fetched and unreasonable to you, but it is my imagination, my fantasy, and my peace. This notion was sealed in my truth, however, when I visited a young psychic medium (Justin Schmoyer) a few months ago.

197

"There are angels in your garden" he proclaimed. I smiled. I knew this.

My daughter, Jessica, pulled up into the adjacent lot and exited the car. I caught a glimpse of her, but the rising sun was particularly bright from her direction, so I motioned with my hand to acknowledge her, then resumed spading and weeding under the shade. At that very moment the door to my house swung open. Peyton stood center of it, hair disheveled and eyes struggling against the glare. Excitedly, she bellowed, "Momma! [slight pause] The doorbell!" Just as she was about to tell us what she heard, it rang again: (DONG-G)....it rang twice!

"I want to hear the doorbell!" Peyton remarked on a dozen or so occasions when the topic came up. "Why won't it ring for me?" she'd say impatiently.

"We have no power over the doorbell, Peyton" I would reply.

"But I want to hear it!" she persisted. "That would totally freak me out if the doorbell rang right now, Nanny!" she pleaded, longingly. In Peyton's mind, there was nothing her Nanny wouldn't do for her; couldn't do for her.

The significance of the chimes will forever have us scratching our heads with grateful fascination. After Sue made the decision to stop the chemo and accept the help of hospice, we had some time to discuss our hopes and our fears. We talked freely about life, and after life. This would typically result in playful banter, an interruption to divert an otherwise tearful ending. She looked at me through an ornery smile and said, "You're gonna' miss me when I'm gone."

Without hesitation, I remarked, "Yeah, right, like you're not going to come back and haunt me for the rest of my life!'

She snickered and said, "Yeah, I've got to have Mom teach me how to ring the doorbell."

"Ugh...Seriously?" I paused emphasizing the humor, then bounced back. "Well, if you're going to ring the doorbell, can you make sure you ring it twice, so I know it's you and not your Mother?"

"Okay!" She said as though it would be no challenge at all.

Never, ever in the 5-year history of this doorbell phenomenon had the doorbell chimed more than once...until the morning after her passing; until her little girl could be there to hear it. There, indeed, was nothing that her Nanny wouldn't do for her, even beyond this earthly life.

Though we never talked about it, it had become evident throughout the course of Sue's illness the doorbell seemed to signal less than joyful news. What it did foretell, each time, was another challenge; another hurdle. This was a two-sided revelation, though, because aside from the unsettling nature of what lied ahead, it offered Sue a sense of comfort. She truly believed the bell to be a sign from her mother "*I'm here, Sue. I'm here with you.*"

When the entire, horrific ordeal had ended...when the bell rang twice, I truly believed it too.

Peyton's spirit lifted, and I silently uttered my gratitude to the Universe for allowing Sue to fulfill another dream on our granddaughter's behalf.

Within a week, I called my psychic medium friend, Justin, who agreed to see me. I'd been to Justin on a couple of occasions over the years and his demeanor, complete with soft tone and tempered enthusiasm were equally or more appealing to me than his uncanny talent for connecting with the afterlife. I told no one I was going because I was truly concerned for what he might say and how I might respond. I have complete faith in him, though he'd never met Sue. He held my hand and I spoke my name aloud three times. His technique always leaves me in a bit of a mystified trance. Sue was there, he said, and eager to talk to me.

"She's with an older woman…" he said, and as I was about to offer an assumption, he interrupted before I began. "But it isn't her mother."

"Oh?" I responded curiously. My mind began to swirl with possibilities.

"Excuse me, dear" he said. "Has your Mother passed?"

"Yes" was my reply.

"Yes," he continued, "she's with your mother and they both want you to know this."

My mouth opened in disbelief, and frankly, I didn't believe it.

But then he went on. "I'm getting a sense Sue and her mother had some unresolved issues when they parted this life. This happens, dear…but chances are likely they will be fine. It was your mother who was there to greet her when she crossed over."

"But, what about her Dad?" I asked.

"He isn't present, but there is another man here" he paused "and a dog. They are all playing with a dog, but there are other animals, too."

"Is the dog 'Simi'?" I pleaded. "What man?"

"No, I don't think the dog's name is Simi…" he offered in resignation. "The dog appears to be with your Mother. I think she says his name is 'R-r-r-…' I'm not getting it, but it starts with an 'R' and ends with and 'E' sound.

"Rocky?" I inquired, "Rocky was her grandparents' dog when she was a little girl."

"Rocky" he confirmed, "that's it." I was justifiably blown away.

"But, who's the guy?" I asked, further curious.

"Again, the name starts with an 'R' but, there are two names, and he is referring to you with two names also…"

"Oh my God!" I uttered, astonished; my mouth still open.

My dear cousin, Roger Allen, died in a tragic accident the previous year. He always called me 'Debby Jean'.

Within a few minutes, heaven's gate appeared to open with a plethora of people from my past. Justin named or described each of them. They'd all come to support me, encourage me, and to convince me of their presence…to renounce their absence.

Justin went on to predict some events that made no sense. He asked if I was planning to move. I said 'no'. He said he saw me in a different home. He saw me standing in a kitchen overlooking trees…a living room with a fireplace. He told me to write. He said people would find value in the telling of my experiences. He said to expect some problems with my left knee and not to delay getting attention for it, and with further regard to my health, I would have some problems in my mid-section. "It is your mother who tells me this," he said. He promised Sue would contact me often, and that she wasn't the only one. "You're surrounded by spirit" he said once again, and I was never more certain of it.

Within two years I had my left knee replaced, and within weeks of my healing, I began to bleed internally. Apparently, my adrenal glands (in the mid-section) took issue with the blood thinners prescribed me post knee surgery.

"Pay attention to numbers because they are of special value to you, and when you see three sevens, note that something of concern is about to manifest, but you will be okay."

I was trying desperately to keep up with his predictions; still pondering the 'spirit' remark.

"You mentioned 'spirit'," I said. "Are spirits and angels the same thing?"

He was so excited to continue, he seemed to ignore my question.

While people tend to use the terms for these two entities interchangeably, they are not the same. Spirits are considered the consciousness of persons who have transcended the human experience. Angels, on the other hand, are superior to spirits in that, they have never been human. Angels are most commonly employed to assist spirits during transition into the spirit world, and while capable of working in the same capacity of spirits, it is rare (but not impossible) for angels to manifest in this manner.

"I know this sounds kind of weird" he said, "but, Sue is showing me an owl on a tree limb...she says to tell you every time you see one, she is with you."

Unlikely, since I lived in the city and trees were a bit scarce.

My head spun and I ached to know more, but he was limited for time and told me my intuition wouldn't let me down. "If you think there is a sign," he said, "there is."

As we stood to hug and leave, Justin got a very surprised look on his face. "Who is Rosemary?" he said.

"Rosemary?" I replied, equally perplexed. "Rosemary is a friend of ours. She and her partner, Deb, have been checking in on me, but I don't know..."

He offered a surprised look, then said "Sue says she's good for you."

"Really?" I replied. "Okay." I wasn't sure what any of this meant, but I was sure it meant something. I didn't know what my next move was, either, but I decided to pay more attention to my surroundings; to give more reverence to what God put in place for me. Instead of relying on right or wrong, I've tried to rely more on what my circumstances offer...what they mean.

The Universe validated me. It fostered my imagination and strengthened my faith. In fact, I wondered *how close were the two?* I discovered that (for me) my imagination is an integral ally to my faith and maybe even one in the same sometimes. Only I can truly know when. Perhaps my imagination is the unique way in which the Universe chooses to communicate with me. Once again, I felt delivered. Once again, I felt I was right where I was supposed to be...and at the right time. I needed to honor the messages and to trust my faith.

CHAPTER 20

The weeks and months...

...after Sue's death were both challenging and enlightening. We held two memorial services, one doubling as a benefit for the Ortenzio Cancer Center where Sue made weekly visits over during her final four years. Friends and family gathered, bands played, and pictures doubling as videos automatically looped on the wall substituting as a screen. There were over 100 people gathered in the activities room of the Penbrook United Church of Christ, the weather accommodating. Food was prepared and donated by various friends; decorations were provided and perfectly placed by our children, accented by an incredible display of photographs of days gone by, memories eternal. Smiling and still faces; proof of life...proof of presence.

Our son-in-law, Mike, sang one of Sue's favorites: *"Somewhere Over the Rainbow"*. His mother, Marie, sang a couple hymns and Janie Womack, a tenured friend and guitarist perfectly captured the tone of the event with uplifting and heart-filled songs. Balloons filled with helium were situated at each table amongst the flowers and picture books situated as centerpieces. Sue's brother Larry and his family, and each of our children and grandkids meandered from table to table to gently exaggerate stories of their mother, grandmother and cherished friend. There were doctors and nurses and a minister, too, each with a favorite 'Sue' story to share. There was laughter and tears.

I took a deep breath and stood to acknowledge everyone; and to give a toast to a woman who left an indelible mark on the hearts of all of us:

"It hasn't been too hard to come up with a speech that truly touches on Sue's nature. She was cranky, and she was loved, and she was pretty proud of her ability to drive the rest of us crazy. She was often difficult and always complicated. There is not one other living person capable of comfortably wearing her shoes. She had a size and a style all her own.

Our personalities were as different as night and day. I'm pretty sure we were compared to oil and vinegar on more than one occasion. But whatever it was that drew us to one another in 1993 never let us go. We certainly encountered some trying situations. One might guess we were not the definitive example of the term 'soul mates' given the way we fought through most of them. Separately and together, our notions about life and love were vastly dissimilar. Through the snarled web of those threads that united us though, we eventually, and painstakingly, untangled privately held dreams and fears deep within each of us. From there, a sprout...a blossom...a becoming. Sue and I allowed each other the space and the support to reach beyond our limitations. We did not suppress those urges. We both grew, certainly, but not in the same direction. I think this was God's plan. It was as though he found two women who no-one else knew what to do with; then, put them (us) in situations to find elusive meaning and purpose.

I was incredibly fortunate to have her in my life, to have her at my side. She was my defender and my protector, my lover and my best friend. By virtue of my life with Sue, I inherited some amazing gifts. Her friends and family may have been a little skeptical with me at first, but Sue kept pushing me down their throats. You might say she won. You might be more correct to say that I won. The fact is they continue to let me lean on them when I need to feel her presence. As our friend Nicole said to me recently, "we all have a little bit of Sue in us, Debby, if we're lucky." Small doses, though, for the sanity of us all, please...small doses.

Sue stretched the boundaries of all her relationships, and she hurt deeply for some of that. If you hurt Sue once, though, you rarely had an opportunity to do it again. She could and would change her mind, at times, but without interference or influence. Sue doled out unconditional love....and expected no less in return. In this one defining way, she was all in.

She did judge people, sometimes too quickly, but almost always with the uncanny ability to be right about their character. She was not a bigot. There was no discerning judgment as to your culture, the color of your skin, your socioeconomic status, or your religious beliefs. Unlike me and perhaps unlike you, she had a sixth sense that picked up on the socio-pathologies of people within minutes, or even seconds. She was right more often than she was wrong about their behavior.

Whenever I suffer one of those moments doubting the kind of person I am, I remind myself 'Sue liked me, so I must be okay.'

As a child in elementary school, Sue would speak of her relationships with those children socially chastised for one reason or another. She was proud of the person she was...unapologetic. Her kindness and compassion were largely due to her upbringing, but she could not help but take the extra step and seek out with a vengeance those castigating peers on the serving end of unfair torment. It was nothing for her to 'get in somebody's face' to stand for the underdog. This was a lifelong truth. In all cases where mutual respect came into play, if you were befriended by Sue, you were a friend for life. She had a lot of friends--damn good ones.

She earned and deserved the honor these people bestowed upon her. She taught us the real meaning of loyalty.

If you truly knew Sue, you couldn't deny her unforgiving temper. She was impulsive and sanctimonious. Every unrestrained reflex told the recipient everything they needed to know for going into battle with her – *DON'T!* She looked for trouble with the notion that she had the power to right whatever was wrong. She didn't need muscle strength; only conviction and a commanding attitude. She didn't win every fight, but she never went down without one. She passed that same conviction on to a couple of her grandchildren.

Sue had O.C.D. In this case, the acronym stood for Obsessive Cleaning Disorder. I did not have this condition, but I was expected to develop it. Quickly. She had little patience for clothes being on the floor, shoes being anywhere but in the closet, or dirty dishes laying in the sink. When I cooked, she stood over me with a dish rag. When I cleaned, she cleaned after me. When I argued that I just couldn't take it anymore, she provided me with proof that I could, and would, take more. Laundry was an everyday chore, and so was vacuuming. Occasionally, she would take some time to sit and relax, but not without her dust rag. She had a very deep and soulful connection with her dust rag. *I was rather jealous of that tattered old cloth.*

She was also fearless. On one occasion, someone pulled up to our front porch in the middle of the night and stole our air conditioner. We heard the noises of scraping metal across the wooden frame and Sue lunged for the bedroom window to witness a very large man putting the monstrous appliance in the back of his red pickup.

We were on the second floor. While I ran for the phone, Sue ran after the truck.

At 2:00 a.m.

In her t-shirt.

Without her pants.

She needed, always, to be in the driver's seat. Literally. Wherever we went, she felt the need to drive. I did not argue because, well, by now, you understand why. Yet, I cannot recall a single opportunity where a problem with another driver did not arise. She honked her horn, screamed and waved obscenities, and repeated her disapproval for nearly everyone who dared to be on the road when she was. On those 'rare' occasions that she (herself) made a driving error, it still wouldn't be her fault....*not really*...she was either lost, or in a hurry, or hadn't had enough coffee that morning. How could she possibly be held responsible for those unforeseen circumstances?

She was fiercely protective of her family, her community and her privacy.

On another occasion, a car screeched to a halt in front of our home. A man and his female passenger jumped out of the stopped car amidst a hurricane of verbal assaults. The young man grabbed the woman and pinned her against the frame of the car door. Rather than scare the lady, it seemed to infuriate her. She launched taunting profanities his way. Before I could get my arms around Sue to stop her, she was out the door. "Hey!" she yelled. She did not receive a response. "HEY!" she yelled louder. They looked at her, incredulously.

"You wanna fight?" she screamed, her index finger thrusting upward as to emphatically demand a time-out. "Take it to your own damn neighborhood!" She screamed with such conviction, the startled young couple stopped fighting, got back in the car and took off. I crawled out from under the table and prayed they didn't come back with a few friends and an assault rifle.

Listen, folks, sometimes it was all I could do to keep her from getting us all killed.

You're welcome.

She complained a lot. *Okay, always.* It was just so difficult for her to be satisfied with what she had, more to feel cheated about what she didn't. It seemed we were always 'going at' this topic. Neither of us won the argument and I've come to the conclusion that neither of us were right, nor wrong. That's the way it was supposed to be. We challenged each other, and as a result, we challenged ourselves. It made each of us better because we were able to take something of value from the other's point of view. In nearly every case, though, I drank from the glass that was half full, and she drank what was left. Her frustration with me might have been alleviated a bit if I'd just have remembered to put the damn glass in the dishwasher when I was finished with it.

How will this world turn without you, Sue?"

To my surprise, the world continued to turn, but had she really left?

"Absence without presence isn't absence at all..." ('There')__Art Duprat, 2015

As for the owl on a tree branch? Later, the day of my reading with Justin, I caught a glimpse of something in my bedroom mirror. Long forgotten, and hidden by the placement of our bedroom television, there it hung on the wall...a painted picture called 'The Lord of the Night' depicting said owl on a tree branch, the eyes of which peered at me through my view of the looking glass. Like Mom and Momma and Terry and all those before her, Sue had been with me all along.

Sue kept in touch in a multitude of ways, dare I say, mostly with airborne messages written on the limbs of trees and the wings of birds and butterflies, but also through music and casual glances...and occasionally in my dreams. When I needed more, though, I simply returned to the bedroom to acknowledge her. Friends, too, kept an eye on me and lifted me, no doubt prompted by subtle reminders from Sue's spirit.

I've lost count of the times my dear friend, Shari, has called me to say, "Everything okay with you?" followed by "Sue keeps 'pinging' me." This is how she references nudges from her old friend and confidante. On more than one occasion, I've received one of these messages just when I needed it most.

For my part, I did my best to learn a little about who I was without Sue. True to the promise I'd made to myself after my mother died, I finished, which gave me the courage to begin again. I kept busy, with no real agenda other than letting the Phoenix of my being rise from the ashes of thoughts that no longer served me. I began to contemplate my place in the world, and to give a little more notice to the significance of it. The Universe seemed to appreciate my efforts. The landscape was brighter. The people, kinder. The sounds of nature sharper...magical. I didn't just walk on the grass...I found joy as the blades coolly and gently tickled my feet. I smelled the roses and tasted the lingering odor of peanuts roasting at Zimmerman's Candy and Confection Store down the street. I felt gratitude rise up and fill the air around me. It was a good start, and soon, my senses manifested into something greater. A great collaboration was

211

in effect between me and a higher consciousness. I felt life to be new once again. The acknowledgement of the experience left me to feel a bit silly, at times and was, at first, quite awkward...but signs of encouragement kept my willingness to move forward in check. I kept reminding myself to look toward the light. It held power and purpose, beauty and peace, and the spirits of all those who left this earth before me.

Once found, it devoured me, and I, it. It had a mysterious pulling power, subtle yet persistent, patient and reassuring. There was no fear of failure and no desire to escape. Failing was of no consequence for it would land me in no worse a circumstance than I'd already endured. It beckoned a response, the result of which gave me the power to take each additional step. New thoughts began to unfold, literally from the ethers, and never with a sense of fear. Mysterious sights and sounds became a welcome part of my worldview, providing opportunities for more. I felt lighter and wiser with each step. The Universe was doing most of the work, but I was no longer just a spectator. I didn't have to outshine the light; I needed only to meet it...to accept it.

~

Today.

"Debby…" a soft, but firm voice startles me from deep sleep. I open my eyes. Nobody there, but I smile and welcome it. "Good morning" I mutter, feebly. My voice is crusty.

I close my eyes and try to force sleep to return, but there is an air of expectation present. I struggle to meet it …this curious urge that lacks direction. Something is begging my attention, but it is out of reach; unclear. I wonder if the menagerie of my mind is teasing me again, or if this is the tail of an unfinished dream, an interruption, produced internally or from somewhere outside of my consciousness. My mother's words seep through the lucid clouds of my memory. "Earth to Debby" is how she might summon me from my stupor. I conjure up another half-hearted smile just thinking about her and the frustrations she suffered with the undisciplined way I managed my world.

Pulling myself upright is a chore; cobwebs of deep sleep are prevalent, and I labor to clear my head. It is difficult to acquaint myself to this intrusion…to form it or to capture it, but I am excited for it, nonetheless. I sit on the edge of my bed and stare limply at the breaking dawn. Frustration begins even as I push away from it. *Patience,* I silently caution myself, *just wait.* I close my eyes.

I settle in place with a deep breath and put together the words of my newly discovered morning (Sanskrit) mantra, "So Hum, So Hum" just as the rising sun introduces herself into my awareness. *'It will come"* I resolve, as I temper my energy. Then, *"Don't force it',* just above a whisper as I try to corral the thoughts racing from the weather-ridden gate of my mind. *'Be still'* I repeat once and again.

213

"So-o-o Hum-m-m…"

Birds in my backyard are playing. The wind is howling, and the window glass seems to heave and exhale to the uneven gusts of cold Canadian air. The Lord of the Night looks at me and I think I see him wink at me. I wink back.

I love my new home. Complete with a fireplace and a picturesque view, I am no longer in the city. It has been over 18 months since Sue's passing. 18 months since my introduction to the glory and grace of a new chapter in my life. My partner, Rosemary, is making breakfast and singing to her houseplants. I smile as I listen to her, because it is easy, because it is smile-worthy.

I met Rosemary (Ro) just a year ago. We'd both shown up for a gathering of single lesbian women to watch a concert. By the time my friends canceled, I was already there. Rosemary's date for the evening was a no-show, too. The room was busy with people familiar with one another while I sat paralyzed, uncertain of my surroundings; my back to the wall, afraid to move should someone notice me. I was completely out of my element and spent much of my time just considering opportunities to escape. It was a shaky and nervous start for me, and I had just built up enough courage to peal myself from the chair and sneak out the side door when she appeared in front of me, her wide and welcoming smile a perfect complement to an uplifting aura, her eyes glistening with excitement, just because it was natural for her. We talked the entire evening, a light of comfort shining in the distance between us. We exchanged information and left. There was little doubt for the source of this accidental meeting. Apparently, the Universe had more in store for me.

It is nearing the end of (this same) gray January morning. Clouds are stubborn to yield to the sun, and Mother Nature provides the ingredients for a game of "King of the Hill". Blowing winds whistle as they pass through the deck boards on my second-floor balcony. The wind initiates with a shivering surge. Tree branches on the old Northern Pine just behind my apartment flutter and sway, but her bough holds steady.

'HaHa' she seems to say, 'is that all you've got?'

To the north and across the hollow, an assemblage of trees against an otherwise barren and snow-covered hillside applaud with crowded tree limbs. They echo a resounding howl as they absorb, then push back against a brutal squall. Perhaps, they are cheering her on or maybe they are part of the main event. Nonetheless, my eyes hold watch closer to the large evergreen outside my bedroom window. Close by and to her east just a few yards, a Red Maple, naked with abandoned leaves has little to sway and less to say. She appears to be little more than a spectator, perhaps an understudy to the older, more resilient, fir. One might sense she is learning from the master.

The wind picks up and the two trees bend and return. A gust thrashes with fury and a dozen or so birds litter the playground. They are eager to join the festivities, but they know, of course, to ally with the Pine. *She always wins, of course!* They are house wrens mostly, and finches, but the arrival of a male and female cardinal are moments away. This is their pattern; one that I've witnessed time and again. The red birds make use of their daily invitation to this outdoor free-for-all and usually arrive late, but always together. The wind continues...ebb and flow, shudder and crash.

This powerful display continues its endless and powerful volley on every living thing just beyond the glass, and I consider adding another ten minutes of sleep before breakfast.

Not a chance. Right on cue, the red birds land at the base of the tree, just inside the decorative white picket fence bordering a steep knoll. The male pecks at the ground for an occasional snack, but mostly keeps watch while the female moves about and takes full advantage of freshly scattered sunflower seeds. In lieu of returning to bed, I take a seat at my desk and watch the show. I smile and wonder if they sense my pleasure. A woodpecker swoops his way into the event, though his commitment to anything other than the hull of the red maple is questionable. He is quite jittery, as always, but seems otherwise completely disenfranchised with the energy swirling about him. Sculpted blue and white Nuthatches and ever-present Juncos feverishly jump from branch to branch. I enjoy them all and do my best to make them a part of each morning.

During the winter and much earlier in the spring, I can expect their integrated melodies to coincide with my alarm clock around the break of dawn. January is our coldest month here, and days like this, I awaken with great anticipation to the magical power of the sun's cascading splash of color; its onset adding to the beauty of nature's canvas. The aura of each living thing is most vibrant at sunrise. Even the brown sparrows and gray pigeon doves share the aesthetic glow of the sun's early morning rays permeating an otherwise wintry, dull countryside. The majesty of the cardinals gives me pause and wonder. Every single time. But, every feathered child of the Universe looks highlighted in contrast to the dead, brown residuals of a retired autumn landscape.

This scene...this reoccurring theme never disappoints. Most days it is all I need to massage my spirit and lift my soul. These precious moments catapult me to a higher level of joy. Birds too stubborn or too lazy to head south for the winter flutter, frolic and feed in my small back yard. I delightfully provide seed for them throughout the cold months, a measure of gratitude that pales in comparison to the timeless

216

entertainment they render me in return. This morning is certainly no exception.

Out of the ordinary this morning, a large crow enters the mix. He dances gaudily about the snow-littered base of the young Maple, eager to join in on the excitement, or so it seems. But the smaller birds don't welcome him. They stop their play even as the wind challenges their resolve. A swelled gale surges at the larger bird's frame, and I can see his feathers bristle about. Still, the smaller birds steadfastly hold their positions in the swirling wind. It is as though his presence is meant to interrupt their routine. *Or mine?* The blackbird lingers for a moment, leaves a trail of imprints in the softer snow and exits. I am sad for his departure. I don't want him to leave. I sense a familiarity with him, and in this moment, I cannot shake it. "Why?" I mutter aloud. In lieu of a dozen or so other questions pressing for attention, I decide to put my thoughts on the tasks for the day.

One last glance.

Imprints. Impressions. One of the two will be gone by spring.

The mysterious energy returns with a temporary anxiousness. It sneaks up on me without summons. An unending cascade of questions prove unyielding; *'What is it?'* *'Why is it?'* At times like this, I convince myself I possess an unrefined sensitivity, but what am I supposed to do with it? Intuition? Perhaps, but for what? It is a mysterious sensation I have tripped over, fought with, then dismissed, many times in my past. In recent years, I have been most tolerable of its mischievousness, and more patient for it to present itself; even eager! A consequence of age and experience, I guess. I know it will clarify itself. It always does. Ready or not.

It is not lost on me that I have been awarded my yesterdays as a springboard for better tomorrows, and sensitivities, too, for the purpose of fully realizing my existence here. I'm all in. I don't pretend to know why I have been so blessed; provided one chance after another for finding peace and wholeness, real love and happiness. My brother, Terry, for all I know, made one mistake and died as a result. But I've come to believe there is no blame...just a mystery the rest of us continue to chase because we need an explanation to justify our behavior here.

A crease, a memory, a sliver of an opening where curiosity demands more of me; peaceful but not passive...persistent. Where giddiness or sadness or any other of a few emotions surface without invitation and leave me longing for more. When a large black bird unexpectedly and poignantly appears in my backyard, then flies away leaving me with unsettled questions and a feeling of want in my solar plexus, I will strongly consider there is a reason for it...a message, an invitation to follow it wherever it may lead. I breathe in, and exhale slowly. I smile for the wonder of another magical conquest, another opportunity for adventure.

The Universe whispers...'follow me'.

SPECIAL THANKS AND RECOGNITION:

Dr. Gregory S. Willis

Dr. Edward S. Podczaski

Barb Brenize-Hetzel, Sue Sands, and

The Entire Staff of Brave and Beautiful Women

With the Ortenzio Women's Cancer Center in Enola, Pa.

AND

To All the Warriors Under Their Care

About the Author:

Debby Livingston-Jones is from Weirton, W.V. She currently resides in Harrisburg, Pa., with her partner, Rosemary. Despite her diagnosis she loves the outdoors even if she must take extra precautionary measures to experience it. She and her partner enjoy evening hikes, gentle breezes and overcast days, precious time with their grandchildren, friends and family...and Major League Baseball. They practice faith with others of like mind and spirit at the open and affirming Unity Church of Palmyra.

Debby continues to write and is currently working on her first novel. Rosemary continues to encourage her.

Debby is among the oldest of only 350 people affected by XP in this country and continues with treatment at Penn State Hershey Medical Center. She could not have lived to tell her story without the kindness of others. "If you can choose to be anything," she says, "choose to be kind. You might just save a life."

For more information on Xeroderma Pigmentosum, and to donate to children who wish only for the simple pleasure of playing outdoors, please visit;

https://xpfamilysupport.org

Every child deserves a day in the sun. If you can't donate money, donate your ideas for a better life experience. Donate love. Donate kindness. A little goes a long way.

Please consider, also:

Sandy Sprint / Sandy Rohrman Ovarian Cancer Foundation:

Donate: https://secure2.convio.net/srocf/site/Donation2?

Made in the
USA
Middletown, DE